ANNAMARIA FERRAMOSCA

OTHER SIGNS,
OTHER CIRCLES
A Selection of Poems:
1990-2009

Translation and Introduction by
Anamaría Crowe Serrano

Other Signs, Other Circles

ChelseaEditions

Series: Contemporary Italian Poets in Translation, 6

Chelsea Editions, a Press of Chelsea Associates, Inc., a not-for-profit corporation under section 501(c)(3) of the United States Internal Revenue Code, has the support of the Sonia Raiziss Giop Charitable Foundation.

Cover photo: Bibliotheca Alexandrina nova, 2008, by Annamaria Ferramosca
Covers & book design: John Stahle Graphic Design (johnstahlegraphicdesign.com)

Library of Congress cataloging-in-publication data:

Annamaria Ferramosca, 1946
Other Signs, Other Circles: A Selection of Poems: 1990–2009
Annamaria Ferramosca, translated by Anamaría Crowe Serrano, p. 225

ISBN–13 978-0-9823849-2-3
ISBN–10 0-9823849-2-0

1. Ferramosca, Annamaria—Translation into English
2. Crowe Serrano, Anamaría, 1957– II. Title

Manufactured in the United States of America by Thomson-Shore, Inc.

First Edition 2009

Chelsea Editions
Box 125, Cooper Station
New York, NY 10276-0125

www.ChelseaEditionsBooks.org

ChelseaEditions

CONTENTS

CONTENTS

CONTENTS

CONTENTS

INTRODUCTION

The 61 poems gathered in this collection were written between 1990 and 2009 and as such they span the length of Annamaria Ferramosca's poetic journey. They stand here in chronological order of publication, which began with *Il versante vero* (Fermenti, 1999), followed by *Porte/Doors* (Edizioni del Leone, 2002) which was published in bilingual form with translations by Riccardo Duranti and Anamaría Crowe Serrano, then *Curve di livello* (Marsilio, 2006), while the final section of this book contains previously unpublished poems.

The advantage of collating the work of 20 years under one title is that it allows us to observe the poet's evolution as she hones her craft. Ferramosca's poetry is unique in an Italian context. While her work is obviously informed by an established canon, it can't easily be said to belong to any in particular. There are elements of Neo-Orphism in some of her work, in the heavy reliance on the evocative quality of the word, but at times she also rubs shoulders with the Mytho-modernist movement, using language that transcends the moment and looks to the future in search of a collective cosmic conscience which might enable humankind to communicate more effectively and understand itself better. While she makes token obeisance to the -isms around her, she doesn't conform to the automatic writing of any particular -ism. Her work is properly independent, both lyrical and experimental, pursuing a very personal thematic and linguistic inquiry of her own. It is an individual voice which was already evident in her first collection.

One word that comes to mind on reading Ferramosca's

poetry is movement. Wherever her poems begin, by the end of the poem, the reader has been transported elsewhere. With each collection she publishes, this phenomenon becomes more pronounced, as if she deliberately explores further and further afield, opening doors onto the world to highlight the fact that there *is* a world out there in which everything is inter-related and inter-dependent, and has been for millennia. The overall effect is of embarking on an odyssey through landscapes which are familiar to us, but which she transforms into a vibrant, fantastical land of revelations, unveiling the hidden truths in words, objects, encounters and events, as well as possible solutions to the problem of fragmented communities and environmental devastation.

The journey is rarely easy for the poet, and this is reflected in her language which, at times, rejects the easy path to interpretation, especially in her later work. Sometimes it is a personal journey, as in the very moving poem, "Had I had daughters", traveling through domesticity, but Ferramosca usually goes beyond the personal to the geographical, cultural, scientific and linguistic, with consciousness evolving from the local to the global. Dialectic variations in pronunciation, for example ("*lu rusciu de lu mare*", Mediterranean) or references to local customs (Mary on Good Friday and Piazza of the defeated tarantulas), rather than self-referentially evoking the charm of small communities, recall the wider context of Italy's history and delve at the same time into issues of universal import - the environment, genetic engineering, social deprivation, tolerance and harmony between people. In fact, she comfortably transgresses the most controversial of poetic boundaries into the world of science (which is her professional domain), highlighting a language not usually associated with things poetic. They are refreshing and revealing incursions. As a scientist, she is brave enough to acknowledge the limitations of the discipline and for years she has been preempting the suggestion that science needs to "make the poetic leap from measurement and analysis to meaning and synthesis".[1] There are few contemporary poets who are as perfectly positioned to make that leap.

Ferramosca is constantly honing her technique, never eschewing the opportunity to experiment. A favorite device, which is by now one of her hallmarks, is the composites she makes of two, sometimes three words ("technocrown", "bloodlymphhumus", "languagesilence") which symbolically embrace one another, erasing the emptiness between them. The fact that everything in the universe comprises matter as well as empty space is paramount to Ferramosca's thought. We are nothing in the greater scheme of things. And at the same time, we are everything although, crucially, we have little idea of exactly how or where we stand within the complexities of consciousness and subconsciousness.

Equally, and paradoxically, she splices words ("sha-king") to expand their range of reference. Through word repetition she produces incantatory tones that can, on occasion, acquire a tantric quality reminiscent of primitive poetry, which gives her words great energy and momentum. Her poems are often peppered with foreign words, too, taking them right out of a personal arena into a more global context. And, in fact, this seems to be the aim of much of Ferramosca's work: to reach out through language, tame the complexities of her interior monologue so as to make vital connections with the world. The passion with which she pursues her aim is evident in the rigor of her language and the diversity of theme. Intensely conscious of the dichotomies that are at the root of all being, Ferramosca knows that the word can be powerful

One word alone
can murder, just
One note
can silence a violin

(To speak as if being born)

while conversely, "[t]he true word is born of silence". We need to learn to listen to the planet and to ourselves, hear the meaningful moments of convergence in order to appreciate that everything in the universe is intricately linked.

Silence
A wait for fusion
Or for another mystery, seeing
as we are already
a claywatery shadow

(Silence)

Naturally, the work stands on its own as ink on paper, but it is enhanced when Ferramosca reads her poetry aloud. A poet's unique interpretation of his/her work always adds nuances that the reader might completely overlook. (It can, of course, sometimes change the meaning of what is read in silence.) Moreover, the gestation of the written word is the poet's inner voice, whether spoken or unspoken, before it ever hits the page. Ferramosca is very conscious of this, of the musicality of words (the first stanzas of "Lullaby wrong way round" should be sung, for example, in a slightly lilting voice, switching to monotone once the poet starts "Losing / the lyrics"). It is worth mentioning that her reading voice is haunting and druidic, very much in keeping with the solemnity of ancient ritual that is referenced throughout her work. But nothing is over-played. There is no drama or gimmick in the performance, just as there is none in the poems themselves. It is voice, pure and simple, revealing a genuine, almost spiritual concern with ecological, social and mythical themes, and profound distress at the inevitable negative impact on society if we ignore the poetic psyche that connects us to the universe.

1. Il Versante vero (The True Side of the Mountain)

Despite being a biologist by profession, Ferramosca has always been very conscious of her poetic calling as a more authentic way of engaging with the world around her. She believes passionately in the possibilities poetry offers for probing deeper into issues which science sometimes leaves unexplained. This began with the publication of *Il versante vero*, a collection in which she expanded her scientific enquiry to explore the path of poetic investigation, climbing a metaphorical mountain side of a very personal nature. The act of writing (good) poetry demands brutal honesty. It demands journeying to a place where the poet surrenders to the challenges of self and the world and faces whatever demons he/she might find there, grappling with them without being assured of the outcome. Ferramosca doesn't shirk this challenge. Repeatedly, she strips herself of the baggage of modernity, science, commerce, gently nudging the reader to do likewise, and returns constantly to places where human dignity and the dignity of the word are restored. She knows that this is the only way it might be possible for her

[….] to survive
empty life works
Yield
to real fires.

(Sometimes you see)

In fact, rebirth, returning to one's origins, to innocence, or childhood, ultimately unlearning what has been learnt, as a way of shedding the trappings and prejudices in life that distract us from what really counts, are all recurring themes throughout these poems. The poet is at times "a mother who must unmother" (Detaching), at times an observer of nature, keenly aware of the constant process of renewal required to reach maturity and fulfil the life-cycle.

I watch water. I learn
how to evaporate,
how exuviae are abandoned

(I watch water)

Of the three collections Ferramosca has published to date, *Il versante vero* is the most thematically diverse, reflecting the poet's personal concerns (Detachment), sociological observations (Istanbul), everyday encounters (Stranger on a plane). Rarely does Ferramosca refer to her work as a nutritional biologist, but there is one exception here (You've been devoured by the world), not repeated in any other collection. It is a significant poem in that it ends with an urgent hope that the poet, in her capacity as a nutritionist, might save the patient from herself by harnessing some primitive instinct.

every day some sea drowns you
every night some sky dreams of me
I the dolphin's back
at your shore.

Key to this "dream" of a solution, is a return to a state of consciousness that has not been corrupted by civilization. It is a theme that is reiterated in later collections. One of these uncontaminated states is to be found in childhood, epitomized in the musicality of the poem "Lullaby wrong way round", where innocence is seen as the purest way of looking at the world and childhood as having the strongest and most unbiased grip on life.

The importance of the child's untainted world view has parallels in the return to ancient traditions and rituals performed in local communities, particularly in Southern Italy, where Ferramosca is from. But the focus is never merely descriptive or folkloric in tone. As always in her poetry, there is strong symbolism at work behind apparently simple acts. The taranta, a lively traditional dance, is the highlight of many village festivals in Southern Italy and is learnt by locals from an early age. The reason for it being named after the tarantula is unclear. It has been suggested that the dance developed as a result of people being bitten by the spider and needing to vigorously shake off its poison. What is relevant here (and in references to the spider in later poems) is that Ferramosca uses the spider as a metaphor for suffering, solitude, poverty, lack of freedom, everything that we would wish to banish from our lives, and the dance is the symbolic cure.

By unleashing the dancing spirits, in unison,
we exhaust fear

(Piazza of the defeated tarantulas)

2. Porte/Doors

Ferramosca's second collection, *Porte/Doors*, was given a bilingual airing from the start. Published in 2002, the poems appeared with accompanying translations which were the result of a collaborative process between Riccardo Duranti and me. I have left some of the original translations untouched but have taken the opportunity to modify others, sometimes substantially.

One of the pleasures of this project for me has been going back over old material and making new discoveries, seeing familiar lines of verse take on new meaning. And meaning, for Ferramosca, is the raison d'être of the poem. The poem must communicate and what it communicates is unconscious truths. As she becomes more confident in her linguistic enquiry, she takes greater liberties, always careful not to transgress the dignity of the word as it uncovers "the hidden sense of things", the mysteries of life. As ordinary language becomes increasingly inadequate as a mode of expression, the poet calls for new perspectives on language, new ways of speaking that might prove more ethical and efficient, allowing us to wipe our slate clean, erase the damage that has been done through the ignominious use of language over the centuries and begin afresh. In "To speak as if being born", she awaits this new voice the way an expectant mother might await the unborn child, its innocence, and the peace evoked by the Brandenburg Gates.

To speak as if
being born to others, every time
born
into the white light where
whiteness is the universe offered by the notes
the buzzing angels over Berlin
over regions
outside doubt outside misunderstanding
This is how children speak kneading the earth
with the least pain needed

In this second collection Ferramosca begins to seriously, and with remarkable ease, work scientific concepts into the poems. The enviable corpus of knowledge at her fingertips breathes new life in a poetic context. Ferramosca believes wholeheartedly in the convergence of disciplines, languages and people as the way forward in a world where meaningful connections seem to be rapidly unravelling. The process of hybridization that she very often refers to in the poems "confusexcites" her. She thinks nothing of intimately embracing what to most people would seem manifestly unpoetic topics, ("genetically modified organisms" or "polycyclic aromatic hydrocarbons"), and can convincingly exploit the scientific idiom in a way that enriches both poetry and science. Her understanding of biology enables her to treat her subject with surprising originality, personifying molecules (in Polycyclic Aromatic Hydrocarbons) as "ancient friends", "petroleum souls" and "companions…/ in our journey towards dust".

The wealth of imagery in these poems and the novelty of Ferramosca's approach prompts us to think beyond any one discipline at a time, so that we discover a fusion of genres, events, philosophies and systems which cause us to examine the familiar afresh.

The emblematic doors of the title open on to the world, allowing us to gaze on situations, places, suffering, the dangers of rampant technological and scientific progress, and love – always love as the route to universal harmony.

3. Curve di livello (Contour Lines)

In Ferramosca's third collection we begin to see a more structured thematic approach. The focus here is on encounters between people who start out disconnected from one another, emotionally, psychologically, geographically, like points on an ordinance survey map which are then linked by the contour lines which are at the imaginative centre of this collection. The cartographic metaphor represents a call for unity and solidarity. As always in Ferramosca's work, dialogue is the key to achieving this. Many of the poems speak of the efficacy of the word, its importance as a way of bringing people together, and understanding cultures. The word, in whatever form it takes (written on paper, carved on rock, "voicesong"), is intense, almost sacred, containing the power "to unveil time" from which we can learn. But we can also use it actively, "to say no / to death inflicted by man".

The kind of solidarity the poet envisages appears in the geometric metaphor of the circle, (sometimes referred to as clearings) which almost always harks back to the gatherings of primitive people around communal fires, often sharing bread. (Analogies in the scientific world, where human beings are at the centre of consciousness of the universe, cannot be dismissed.) For Ferramosca, the simplicity of the earliest humans represents a way of life based on sincere, less superficial communication. She attempts to tap into their consciousness, in particular their social co-operation and peaceful ways of life. Concurring with the work of the archaeologist Marija

Gimbutas, Ferramosca believes in the strongly positive feminine influence in these primitive cultures. She transposes the idea of Neolithic Goddess worship to the present, exalting women for their holistic and practical approach to many of the obstacles that hinder their progress, while at the same time undoing some of the views of women that have traditionally male origins. Romantic idealizations of woman are brought crashing down (passively, of course) with dollops of homemade feminist irony. Eve wanders in the Garden of Eden, bored out of her mind by

> the same old
> bed of flowers, the same old
> overflowing perfume
> Nausea.
>
> (Eve – Eden diary)

Woman in Ferramosca's poetry is all flesh and blood, capable of tenderness and love, infinite versatility. She is both "[v]ulnerable and strong", qualities which provide her with a way of overcoming male aggression and self-importance. There is no hyperbole in Ferramosca's approach to feminist concerns. She speaks quietly, gently advocating love and understanding, as if raising her voice would be a hostile act, despite symbolically screaming at centuries of misconceptions and misrepresentations of woman.

Needless to say, the urge to scream cannot and must not always be repressed. Sometimes the wounds of the world are too painful (as they are in "On disc") and words are, yet again, inadequate, though Ferramosca always returns to these, often chanted or sung, as our ultimate route to peace and healing.

The overriding tone of all of Ferramosca's work, however,

is unassuming. She stands back from her vast scientific knowledge and contemplates the world in awe, humbly asking questions from the Socratic viewpoint of ignorance, which is the best point from which to start learning. So the poet prompts us back to the beginning, to

> the ancient vortex, calm, millennial sails
> returns that turn to farewells
> odysseys bound for other seas
>
> (After Rilke's eighth elegy)

Here we have the journey, about to begin with sails, as it often does in Ferramosca's work, where we can cast off judgements and jaundiced views, acquired knowledge, and imitate the innocence of animals "who know nothing of death".

4. The unpublished poems

As Ferramosca's work matures, her language becomes more complex syntactically and richer in metaphor. The evocative power of the word is called on to a greater extent. Less grammatical constraints facilitate the free flow of thought, creating moments of stream of consciousness which can capture a sense of mystery, leaving greater room for interpretation from the reader. She continues to invent "xtrange" words, now playing with lexicography in a techno-linguistic fashion. Sometimes "[t]he mind / - not having asked for a prosthesis - / boggles" ("xtrange structures").

Syntactic ambiguity deliberately merges with the occasional non sequitur, jolting the rhythm of the line, highlighting lacunae in society's ability to communicate and understand. The most compelling instances occur in "a languagesilence", an intense and dramatic poem which elaborates on earlier themes, rejecting war through a symbolically sacrificial gesture which, once again, has its origins in ancient customs.

> we'll return naked to naked earth
> be the lamb's throat a thousand times over
> should blood be required once more
> to drip slowly to an end

Similarly, enlightenment can be achieved by returning to "the / innocent inside, bloodlymphhumus" (inside being used here as a noun) where meaning and solutions to conflict can be found without the use of violence, "without / metal that might resound".

In general, there is a more concentrated focus on contemporary circumstance in these poems. A sense of unease permeates many of them, disappointment with the duplicity of technology which promises so much on the one hand, yet leaves us unsure of ourselves and emotionally sterile on the other, with "*emoticons* / replacing word-caresses on my skin", threatening a "technodeath" (A forest breeze blows on my cheeks). There is a lament for the loss of home and those metaphorical "circles of words" (Villageworld) that are so important in giving us a sense of community and identity. Even in the title of this poem, any possible gap between the small village and the wider world is eliminated, as the local becomes global and both merge into one and the same thing. Nonetheless, whatever might be lost by the displacement of people, words and the act of writing always provide a way of recognizing meaning all around us. They continue to protect and provide a grounding point of reference.

tattooed home-village that walks with us
everywhere, under the one sky inscribed with stars

(Villageworld)

New to these more recent poems is an impending sense of death, both the poet's and the death of others or of the world, though Ferramosca often avoids explicit mention of it by using extended metaphors, as in "At the first stop", where obvious parallels are drawn between the bus journey and the journey of life. Yet, there is little pathos in these poems despite the fact that

...we spin
on the border between desert and an insolent
land of promises, made sterile
by an excess of sorrow

(They call it living)

The poet is sustained by friends, be they real or imaginary friends from her Etruscan heritage. Once again, she restores deep emotional connections which are the redeeming force in life. She keeps faith with the mysteries of the universe by turning to ancient customs and classical mythology, recalling a time when poetry ruled as the primary oral tradition. Her identity is often closely interwoven with the customs of her female ancestors, where their non-violent attitudes and traditions find a place in the present that might make life more wholesome and authentic.

we etruscan women today, side by side
liquefying all the iron of swords
in exorcistic bowls
and word upon word we model
life into living forms:
stakes for the vineyard, chairs
                    for night-time stories

(we etruscan women)

Ferramosca's research and focus on primitive peoples, her concern for the oral and written word in all its intriguing varieties (exemplified in the cover photograph of this anthology), makes her poetry the closest Italian version of ethnopoetic that I've come across, rich in references to female fertility, sexuality and motherhood.

Ferramosca exploits an incredible wealth of imagery and poetic associations, many of them strongly feminine and mythological, to merge past with present in order to highlight the continuity of physical and metaphysical life and to underscore the more worrisome aspects of so-called progress in the world. She transposes classical references to a very contemporary context. "[L]ittle Ariadnes" playing hopscotch in the street will become "mistress of the labyrinth" in adulthood, capable of revealing the right path to follow out of the potential horrors of "the GMO-chimera". Modern man's plight is given a mythological twist as he is forced to flee to colder climates from the fires of global warming. We leave behind us a world in ruins of Trojan proportions, "fathers carried on our backs / Aeneas en route to Antarctica". But Ferramosca is above all faithful to poetic language as a means of transmitting knowledge and thought, and in so doing she becomes a conduit of new idioms and of past cultures. Her poetry is charged with tension and urgency in the light of imminent disaster, which is juxtaposed with a passion for and confidence in life, in the hybridization of peoples and cultures which will free us of prejudice and fear. The depth of her engagement with the world around her necessitates careful engagement with her poetry. The "other signs, other circles" of the title must be sought out and patiently retrieved, digging deep into the past, into language, and into ourselves so as to illuminate our present. These are not facile poems, not for fast, thoughtless consumption. They are poiesis in its truest etymological sense and deserve to be savored, slowly.

Acknowledgements

I would like to thank the poet, Annamaria Ferramosca, for her unflagging patience with my endless questions and the friendship she has so generously offered since we first met; Riccardo Duranti for his collaboration with *Porte/Doors,* as well as his help with first drafts of "Contour Lines", "Kamikaze" and "Planispheres"; Enzo and Manuel Turco for allowing me to share their space and taking the time to solve my technological problems; Anna Maria Robustelli and Tiziana Pagan for their invaluable comments and suggestions; Mark Kealy, for keeping the boat afloat while I was translating; Rachael for getting through the orals and practicals without me; and Michael for not badgering me so often to bring him to the skate park while I was working (or did I just make that up?).

Anamaría Crowe Serrano
Dublin. April 6, 2009

1. Lotts, Tim, "From here to divinity", *The Sunday Times*, London, April 5, 2009.

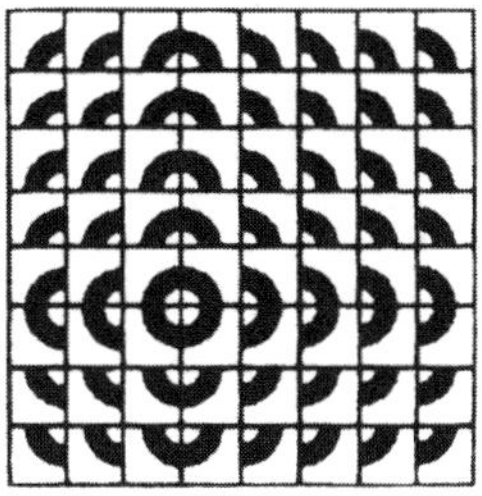

da
IL VERSANTE VERO
(1999)

from

THE TRUE SIDE OF THE MOUNTAIN

(1999)

LA PIAZZA DELLE VINTE TARANTOLE

Abbiamo altre parole questa notte:
un corpo musicale,
a vendicare il tempo
passato senza fuochi
Abbiamo l'alba
che batte su pelli tese in sarabanda,
furore d'argento sugli olivi,
fino al mare - l'eco
ingelosisce le grotte -
Piedi
a scandire colpi d'amore sulla terra
E tuoni
a dissipare tutte le aracnitudini

In piazza l'aria
è disegnata di spade con le braccia
Le ragazze scintillano la terra
dove ballano
Volano i cerchi delle gonne alla luna
S'incendiano i tamburi. Fino a sangue
(A sciogliere i cani ritmici, all'unisono,
si sfianca la paura)

PIAZZA OF THE DEFEATED TARANTULAS

We have other words tonight:
a musical body,
to avenge time past
without fire
We have the dawn
beating a sarabande on taut hide,
a silver frenzy over olive groves,
down to the sea - the echo
making the caves jealous -

Feet
marking the rhythm of love on the ground
And thunder claps
dispelling all aracnitudes

In the piazza arms
sketch the air as swords
Girls make the ground sparkle
where they dance
Skirts in circles fly to the moon
Drums ignite. Till there's blood
(By unleashing the dancing spirits, in unison,
we exhaust fear)

ISTANBUL

Se i minareti allungassero l'ombra
dipanassero fili di garofano blu
fin nei capelli
di questi sciuscià disincantati
vuoiscarpecomestellemillelire
si fermerebbe il tempo
all'angolo vergogna
dell'hotel Mercure.
Franerebbe il tempo
con ali stupefatte
sul tappeto
dei pentimenti.

E Beyoglu
risuonerebbe a un tratto
di giochi e grida
correre a rompicollo
sfidando la prua delle navi sul canale
cercare lungo i fossi
canne robuste
verdi da scortecciare
poi via sul ponte a pescare
uva di Smirne in tasca
fino al tramonto.

ISTANBUL

If minarets lengthened their shadow
unravelled threads of blue carnations
as far as the hair
of these disillusioned shoeshine boys
comeseeyourshoesshinelikestarsforadime
time would stop
at the corner of shame
at the hotel Mercure.
Time would topple
on bewildered wings
to the rug
of repentance.

And Beyoglu
would suddenly resound
with games and cries
a boy running at breakneck speed
racing ships' prows on the canal
searching for sturdy reeds
along the drains
green ones to strip
then
up on the bridge to fish
with grapes from Smirne in his pockets
till the sun goes down.

Vedrebbe il Corno d'Oro
ancora i suoi riflessi
nei capelli vaniglia
nei guizzi all'amo
nei lampi
dell'orgoglio bambino.

A sera affonda
il Gran Bazar dei sogni
in polpa di meduse
sultani smeraldini
come ramarri
dagrandevogliofarecapitanomercantepescatore

Sul cuscino
anice e zafferano.

The Golden Horn would see
its reflections still playing
in his vanilla hair
in the hook wriggling
in the glint
of boyhood pride.

Come evening
the Great Bazaar of dreams
sinks into jellyfish pulp
emerald sultans
like green lizards
whenI'molderIwanttobeacaptainmerchantfisherman

Anis and saffron
on his pillow.

NINNA-NANNA ALL'INCONTRARIO

Dormi
Ti canto il cielo
Ride
con luci piccole, infinite
come le storie piccole del mondo
Spande per te gocce di latte, avvita trottole
Una s'accende, lanterna serena del tuo giro

Dormi
Ti canto il sole
Batte
danze di fuoco accordate
al ritmo del tuo petto
Ma è difficile imitare la musica di un'alba
E tu lo vinci
ché troppo forte è il tuo abbraccio alla vita

Dormi
Ti canto l'uomo
Perdo
le parole. Non so più cantare
Si fa convulso il volo di colombe sul tuo capo
Forse le città troppo scintillano
Troppo alti i fuochi che devastano
Non ricordano di poter scaldare
Si interrompono i ponti. E le parole

LULLABY WRONG WAY ROUND

Sleep
I'm singing you the sky
It's laughing
with little lights, infinite
as the little stories of the world
It pours drops of milk for you, winds up spinning tops
One lights up, a bright lantern for your journey

Sleep
I'm singing you the sun
It's beating
fire dances synchronized
to the rhythm of your heart
It's hard to imitate the music of the dawn
Yet you succeed
your grip on life is that strong

Sleep
I'm singing you mankind
Losing
the lyrics. Can sing no more
The flap of doves over your head is scattered
Maybe cities twinkle too much
The fires of destruction leap too high
Forgetting they can stir warmth
Bridges get interrupted. As do words

Anche se dormi
canta
Tu solo puoi cantare
dalla regione dell'arcobaleno,
ponte comprensibile
che unisce tutti i nidi di colombe
La tua canzone ferma il dio veloce
che inebetisce sguardi
e spegne i fuochi teneri
delle parole
Tu solo li ravvivi,
tu che non smetti
la cantilena noiosa-grandiosa dei perché
Perché i fuochi incendiano, i ponti crollano,
le parole non parlano, perché?
Tu solo, bambino, puoi rispondere

Anche se dormi
cantami l'uomo che sarai
Ti ascolto

Even if you're asleep
sing
Only you can sing
from that region of the rainbow,
that intelligible bridge
that links all doves' nests
Your song stops the fast-paced god
that numbs our gaze
and puts out the tender flames
of words
Only you can revive them,
you who never stop
the tiresome, splendid sing-song of whys
Why do fires burn things down, bridges collapse
words not speak, why?
Only you, child, have the answer

Even if you're asleep
sing me the man you'll be
I'm listening

METROPOLITANA

Uomo e donna, vi guardo.
Tra foglie e nuvole, a tratti,
Eur, Magliana, San Paolo, mi dileguate
quest'aria nera di gallerie romane.
Siete ridenti, oggi, in abiti e parole.
Sulle pareti consunte svaniscono
stratificazioni di pensieri monchi
troppo veloci per sedimentare
o troppo ansiosi d'arrivare
al fondo d'una gioia
o d'un'angoscia.

Siete belli, reali ed inspiegabili
come genesi di mondi.
La stessa grazia di quando maneggiavate l'ocra
nel fumo delle grotte.
E increduli, negli occhi leggevate l'un l'altro
la prima meraviglia dell'arte.
Passavate così, di tempo in tempo
nelle vivide favole.
Poi, da labbra in fogli
con le vostre vicende intessevate
il nostro pensiero inconsapevole.

METRO

Man and woman, I'm looking at you.
Through leaves and clouds, intermittently,
Eur, Magliana, San Paolo, you disperse
this black Roman tunnel air for me.
You smile today, in your dress, your words.
Amputated thoughts stratified
on the shabby walls disappear
too fast to settle
or too anxious to arrive
at some depth of joy
or distress.

You're as beautiful, real and inexplicable
as the genesis of worlds.
The same grace with which you handled ochre
in smoky caves.
And incredulous, you read the wonder of art
for the first time in each other's eyes.
This is how you passed from age to age
into vivid fairytales.
Then, from lips to pages
with your lives you interwove
our unconscious thought.

Così fluisce l'umano mistero.
Brancolando nella profondità dell'atomo
o scrutando gli spazi,
oscuri come queste gallerie
saranno il viaggio e le ultime colonne.
Ma il respiro s'innalza fino al sole, di fuori,
se guardandovi profondi di pensiero e d'amore,
non avverto che luce.

So human mystery flows.
Fumbling in the depths of atoms
or scrutinizing spaces,
the journey and the last columns
will be dark as these tunnels.
But my breathing rises to the sun, outside,
since looking at you deep in thought and love,
all I see is light.

SCONOSCIUTO IN AEREO

L'Olimpo, dall'alto.
Noi, nuovi dei pressurizzati.
Da un quotidiano ellenico
sfogliato da brune dita
si dipana
un magnetico cerchio.
Una eleganza muta
inconsapevole intorno
si disperde in aroma.
E' strano
che solo io la raccolga,
dalla tua alla mia fila
e nel mezzo il destino.
Dalle mani risalgo
su per un torso
di Delo o di Olimpia
verso un profilo assorto
e tremo
nell'Eros dei minimi moti di ciglia.

Sollevi di poco lo sguardo,
quel tanto che basta
a immaginarmi forte la tua storia,
i viaggi i progetti
insieme a...
A una donna extraordinaria
Vorrei dal vero ammirarla
toccata da sorte irripetibile
Andromaca dolce
anche lei di magica stirpe.

STRANGER ON A PLANE

Olympus, from above.
Us, newly pressurized gods.
From a hellenic daily
leafed by brown fingers
a magnetic ring
emerges.
Mute, unassuming elegance
around us
disperses as a scent.
Strange
that only I am perceiving it
from your row to mine
with destiny in between.
From the hands I wander up
a torso
from Delos or Olympia
towards a self-absorbed profile
and I tremble
at Eros, the tiniest quiver of his eyelashes.

You lift your gaze a little,
just enough to allow me
vividly imagine your story,
journeys, plans
together with…
An amazing woman
I'd love to admire her in the flesh
touched by a fate that comes but once
sweet Andromache
she too of the magical lineage.

Insieme a...
figli in tunica bianca
luminosi di geni e di slanci
(ora tenero vira
e giocoso il tuo profilo).

Vorrei solo in un lampo
incontrare i tuoi occhi
e subito
rompere l' incanto
con misere o medie scoperte.
Sedurti, anche poco,
con qualche arcana parola
entrare nel tuo equilibrio
senza rompere il cerchio.
Ma è scritto:
scivoleremo vicini senza un urto.
E l'aereo già atterra.
Non posso
guardare chi ti accoglie.
Mi sgomenta
quel tuo mondo felice
che mi esclude.

Together with…
sons in white tunics
their genes and energy luminous
(now your profile tenderly
becomes more playful).

I'd love our eyes to meet
if only for a split second
and suddenly
break the spell
discover your mysteries or mediocrity.
Seduce you, even a little,
with some mysterious word
enter your composure
without breaking the ring.
But it is written:
we'll brush close without touching.
And the plane is already landing.
I can't look
at whoever's waiting for you.
I'm scared
of that happy world of yours
that excludes me.

LA TUA VITA É UN'ARANCIA

Il tuo arco di vita un incendio, ragazza.
Tieni abbracciato il mondo
coi capelli che cantano!
La tua voce
                    infinita
colora il miniappartamento del mondo.

La tua vita è un'arancia.
Si sgranano gli spicchi.
                                        Volano.

YOUR LIFE IS AN ORANGE

The arc of your life is a blaze, girl.
Hug the world tight
with your singing hair!
Your infinite
                    voice
colors the mini-apartment of the world.

Your life is an orange.
Each segment is pulled out.
                                        Takes flight.

DISTACCO

Oggi sei luna
                    scarmigliata
non ti lasci comprendere
Occhi guizzi di fuga
piccola nave sei
                    disormeggiata
Eppure solo ieri toccavi
il cesto scarlatto dell'abnegazione
offerto da ogni madre

Il non volerti opprimere
diviene in paradosso,
peso o assenza, non so,
                              madre da smadrire
Allora scarnisciti di me,
libera le tue stelle
Va', cavaliere errante, spandi
i tuoi brividi sonori per il mondo,
                                        addentalo
Divorami pure, e pure sputami
So rimanere
pallore d'acquerello al fondale
                                        per il tuo firmamento

DETACHING

Today you are
                    a tousled moon
you resist being understood
Eyes darting towards escape
you're a tiny vessel
                         off its mooring
Yet only yesterday you touched
the scarlet basket of self-denial
offered by every mother

Not wanting to smother you
becomes a paradox,
pressure or absence, I don't know,
                                        a mother who must unmother
So, strip yourself of me,
free your stars
Go, knight errant, spread
your loud shivers through the world,
                                             sink your teeth into it
Devour me, even, and even spit me out
I know how to continue being
the pallor of a watercolor in the background
                                                  for your firmament

TI HA DIVORATO IL MONDO

Arrivi all'appuntamento come
facendoti largo tra le nuvole
coperta di graspi d'uva - venti -
piluccati in minuti - venti - di veleno liquido
in vorace voragine
Ti aspetto
nella stanza dei corrimano gentili
dove scivoli, paziente
sei paziente a correre dietro
i lumini che accendo, i puntelli
che ondeggiano in tumescenze e colpe
nella radura smagliata dei tuoi varchi
dove infuriano i canti
Alti, a sgolarci insieme
a sciogliere i terrori
di nubi fonde e pozzi. Qualcuno
già si chiude, sfiancato.
Ti ha divorato il mondo che divori
ogni giorno mare che t'annega
ogni notte cielo che mi sogna
io dorso di delfino
alla tua riva.

YOU'VE BEEN DEVOURED BY THE WORLD

You arrive at your appointment making
your way through the clouds
covered in grape stalks - twenty -
nibbled in - twenty - minutes of liquid poison
in a voracious abyss
I wait for you
in the room with the kindly handrails
where, patient, you slide
you are patient as you chase after
the little lamps I light, the props
unstable from tumescence and guilt,
in the snagged clearings along your paths
where chants infuriate
Aloud, making us both hoarse
disentangling the terrors
of black clouds and pits. One of them
is already closing, exhausted.
You've been devoured by the world that you devour
every day some sea drowns you
every night some sky dreams of me
I the dolphin's back
at your shore.

ACCADE DI VEDERE

Come incastonata
sulla porta marcita
una falena tremante (un pezzo d'ala falciato
piccola vuota tessera nel mosaico)
aspetta la fine,
beve un ultimo raggio
Sorda agli inviti
sa di obbedire al rito
In bilico dignitoso:
già sugli occhi il velo
che fa opachi i ricordi
già le luci del dopo
sfolgoranti
(celebrano, in lontananza, la festa del patrono)

Ora
rigida e inerme.
"Resisteva anche ai fuochi d'artificio"
appare sulla minima lapide.

Anch'io vorrei resistere
ai vuoti d'artificio
Cedere
ai veri fuochi.

SOMETIMES YOU SEE

As if set
          in the rotting door
a trembling moth (part of its wing cut off,
a tiny missing piece of the mosaic)
awaits its end,
                    soaks up one last ray
Deaf to the invitations
it knows to obey the ritual
With dignified unsteadiness
the veil already across its eyes
                                        blurring memories
already the lights of the afterlife
                                        are dazzling
(from afar they're celebrating the saint's feast day)

Now
       stiff and helpless.
"She survived even fireworks"
is written on her tiny tombstone.

I too would like to survive
                                   emtpy life works
Yield
          to real fires.

FINE

La custodia dell'ombra è terminata
Il mattino dirada sul tuo fianco
pulsazioni di un'enfasi spavalda
L'eco era intensa nella notte
Allentava
ogni mia logora maglia di pensiero
in voragine opaca

Al chiarore ritorni, cavaliere
con promesse fragili e ingrigite
Spesso son le parole a rivelare
l'enorme vacuità delle promesse

Siamo al muro, scoperti
Chiara la sofferenza
Anche il sorriso
Voglia incontrovertibile di fine

END

The vigil over shade has ended
Down your side, morning weakens
the defiant rhythm of your zeal
Its echo was intense at night
It slackened
every threadbare stitch of my thought
into an opaque abyss

At daybreak you return, cavalier
full of flimsy greying promises
Often it's the words that reveal
the huge emptiness of promises

We are exposed, our backs to the wall
Our suffering clear
Our smiles, too
An incontrovertible need for an end

ABBANDONO

Basterà riannodare il filo, Arianna,
dopo l'ebbrezza, e camminare?
Basterà fingersi sorda
se quel rombo il tempo
attutisce in ronzio?
"Segui il filo e continua
- dici - la tua danza

Nuda, come a rinascere, e pure
ebbra, come sei, a ottundere i ricordi"

Il filo sfugge, senza un'ancora
di benevole stelle, e s'aggroviglia.
Forse da sempre sono vestita
di un esile progetto che vacilla

Se mi incontrate, non pronunciatelo
Il mio nome
si è rifugiato in una colombaia

ABANDONMENT

Will it be enough to pick up the thread again, Ariadne,
after the drunkenness, and keep walking?
Will it be enough to feign deafness
if time dulls that boom
to a hum?
"Follow the thread - you say -
and continue your dance

Naked, as if you were being reborn, and even
drunk, as you are, deadening memories"

The thread slips away, without an anchor
of benevolent stars, and gets entangled
Maybe I've always been dressed
in a tenuous plan that wavers

If you find me, don't say it
My name
has taken refuge in a dovecot

SORVEGLIO L'ACQUA

Sorveglio l'acqua. Imparo
come si evapora,
come si abbandona l'esuvie.
In un angolo il mucchio:
il sale della vita (l'acqua è ironica)

Il dio dell'acqua saggio
ondulava in serpente
allevando le spighe
e insieme i pesci
E ignaro, in petto, anche l'uomo.
Tecnica, che solo un dio padroneggia,
ma che esclude
perversioni di plastica.

La sapienza dell'acqua
quando imperla
la fronte per timore,
prima di commettere,
prima di parlare.

I WATCH WATER

I watch water. I learn
how to evaporate,
how exuviae are abandoned.
The pile lies in a corner:
the salt of the earth (water is ironic)

The wise god of water
was undulating like a snake
nurturing the reeds
together with the fish
And man too, unawares, was leeching off him.
It's a technique that only a god can master,
but which leaves no room
for plastic perversions.

How knowledgeable water is
when it covers the forehead
in beads of fear,
before we commit,
before we speak.

GIÀ CHE CORRE LA VITA

Soy hombre: duro poco
y es enorme la noche
Octavio Paz

Già che corre la vita,
scelgo una corsa semplice
Perchè tutto è accaduto
semplicemente
Un soffio
come d'aria che trema
Poi solo
un profumo di menta

Felicità di andare
coi sandaletti nuovi ritrovati
Fermate dolci-amare
abbacinate
sull'incavo di una guancia virile
Correre ancora
gemmare scontrosi rami, non importa
Importa
lasciarsi contagiare dai pensieri,
parole disvelanti
su pagine rubate a mille notti,
rivoli di un' epidemia
scesi a tracciare l'anima

SINCE LIFE IS RACING ON

Soy hombre: duro poco
y es enorme la noche
Octavio Paz

Since life is racing on,
I choose a one-way journey
Because everything has happened
in a simple way
A puff
like trembling wind
Leaving
only the scent of mint

I was happy skipping
in new sandals I'd found again
Dazzled
by bitter-sweet stops
in the hollow of a virile cheek
Running on again,
growing petulant branches doesn't matter
What matters
is allowing yourself to be infected by thought,
revealing words
on pages stolen from a thousand nights,
their rivulets an epidemic
descended to leave a trace on the soul

Al capolinea
ho salvato gli stracci più preziosi,
poche frasi e scarne,
capaci
di guidare il destino
Ora so riconoscere i miraggi
Ora so arrendermi
alle ombre di materia soffribile
Non temo
altri giochi brutali
e cammino
Un cammino placato

Siamo in tanti a scendere
offrendo mantelli ininterrotti
di fuochi e solitudini
Gli orli
son ricamati di domande

At the end of the line
I've saved the most precious rags,
few sentences and meagre ones at that,
capable
of steering destiny
Now I can recognize the mirages
Now I can surrender
to the shadows of suffering
I'm not afraid
of other brutal games
and I walk
A reconciled path

There are so many of us alighting
offering continuous cloaks
of fire and solitude
Their edges
embroidered with questions

da

PORTE/DOORS

(2002)

from
PORTE/DOORS
(2002)

PARLARE COME NASCERE

Voce che inseguo da più notti invano
Ne so bene l'attesa
e l'urto lancinante e l'onda
propagata lungo le strade a nord del cuore
Arriva
ed è squillo di bimba:
- Noi siamo come un violino, vero?
Le parole
volano come la musica dalla bocca
e la lingua è l'archetto...
Ma se piango,
il legno del mio violino è come
un ramo sotto la pioggia? -

Parlare come
nascere agli altri, ogni volta,
venire
alla luce - bianca - dove
bianchezza è l'universo offerto delle note
brusio d'angeli sopra Berlino
sopra le regioni
fuori dal dubbio fuori dagli equivoci
Così i bambini parlano impastando la terra
col minimo dolore necessario

TO SPEAK AS IF BEING BORN

Voice I have been pursuing several nights in vain
I know the wait all too well
and the piercing blow and the wave
propagated along the streets north of the heart
It arrives
and it is the call of a little girl:
- We are like a violin, aren't we?
Words
fly like music from our mouth
and our tongue is the bow…
But if I cry,
is the wood of my violin like
a branch in the rain?

To speak as if
being born to others, every time
born
into the white light where
whiteness is the universe offered by the notes
the buzzing of angels over Berlin
over regions
outside doubt outside misunderstanding
This is how children speak kneading the earth
with the least pain needed

Parlare come
vivere con-dividere
ritmi segreti di qualche dio dei simboli
vibrazioni protette fino a un termine
dove la voce sarà oltremusica
pura illimite
si lascerà
talking about - parlar di tutto
whispering - sussurrare
missing - annullare, perfino
(rumore di rugiada nella notte)

Domani, domani, quando?
Oggi piove
sopra il legno dei rami
Una sola parola
può uccidere, ancora
Una nota
far tacere un violino

To speak as if
living par-taking
in the secret rhythms of some god of symbols
in vibrations protected to the end
where the voice will become more than music
boundless   pure
free to
parlar di - talk about everything
sussurrare - whisper
annullare - miss, even
(the sound of dew in the night)

Tomorrow, tomorrow, when?
Today it's raining
on the wood of the branches
One word alone
can murder, just
One note
can silence a violin

LA MIA PARTE D'ORIENTE

Sotto la pensilina
profumo di tempio
Lei porcellana immobile
distante
distante un mare
distante
un mare del Giappone
inondata
dalle sue pieghe mongole
petalo sottile
tra i rami di un haiku

Anche in occidente
si reputa sconveniente
per una ragazza
prolungare lo sguardo, per strada
su un viso sconosciuto
oltre il flash d'una sillaba

Eppure sotto la pensilina
ho avvertito
per un solo attimo obliquo
piegarsi le sbarre del mondo
penetrare nella mia
una pupilla di seta
mi cercava
- luna dietro le nuvole -
cercava
la mia parte d'oriente

MY PIECE OF THE EAST

Under the bus shelter
                                        the scent of a temple
She, motionless porcelain
                                                far away
far away a sea
                        far away
a sea of Japan
                        flooded
by her Mongolian folds
a delicate petal
between the branches of a haiku

In the West too
it is considered unseemly
for a girl
to let her gaze linger, in the street
on an unknown face
longer than the flash of a syllable

Yet, under the bus shelter
                                                I saw
for a split oblique second
the bars of the world bend over
and a silk pupil penetrate mine
                                                searching for me
- a moon behind the clouds -
                                                searching
for my piece of the East

Solo accostarmi, io nube confusa
ansia di loto
senza sovrapporni
Offrirti le mie figurine immobili
Emily, Simone, Cristina, Amelia
La polpa del mio loto
in cambio
del tuo biancore

I just want to get closer, I, a confused cloud
longing for lotus
without overlapping
To offer you my motionless figurines
Emily, Simone, Cristina, Amelia
The flesh of my own lotus
in exchange
for your whiteness

TI HO DISEGNATO UN SEGGIO

Ti ho disegnato un seggio
e l'ho dipinto ironico
trono di girasoli a-capo-chino
Ti ho immaginato sguardo-nel-fogliame
paralisi stupita delle labbra
domanda fusa al tocco delle dita

E non posso risponderti
ma devo
insolentirti col muso della volpe
intimidirti per l'occhio dilatato
nella consolazione di una sillaba

E giustamente tu ora mostri i denti
alla volpe braccata nel sentiero
delle Parole, fino alla sua gabbia
Impossibile snidarla, impossibile
anestetizzarla
Le ridono intorno sbarre orizzontali
lievi come linee d'orizzonte
(orizzontale e lieve è la scrittura)
Non ti resta
che lanciarle grida d'amore come sassi
nel centro esatto dei suoi cerchi d'aria

I SKETCHED A SEAT FOR YOU

I sketched a seat for you
and painted it as an ironic
throne of sunflowers bowing their heads
I imagined you as a glance-among-the-leaves
as lips in stunned paralysis
a question melting at the touch of fingers

And I cannot answer you
though I must
insult you with a vixen's muzzle
intimidate you with my dilated eye
while I am consoled by a syllable

And in fact you now show your teeth
to the vixen stalked along the path
of Words, right up to her cage
It is impossible to flush her out, impossible
to anaesthetize her
Horizontal bars laugh all around her
light as lines on the horizon
(writing is horizontal and light)
The only thing for you to do
is to throw her cries of love like stones
at the very centre of her rings of air

Dal cuore spicco i semi al girasole
e lego il trono al polso e salgo i cerchi
E rido se ruzzoli dal trono
sparpagliando tutte le mie carte
anche tu in midriasi pupillare
parola ti dilata in canti e stelle

Così mi segui. Il sogno è un Librocielo
Noi sotto un planetario di manoscritti

I pick the sunflower seeds from its heart
and tie the throne to my wrist and climb the rings
And laugh if you roll off the throne
scattering all my cards
even you with mydriasis of the pupil
while the word dilates you into songs and stars

That's how you follow me. The dream is a Sky-book
We, under a planetarium of manuscripts

E MENTRE ESCI DAL BAR

E mentre esci dal bar
addenti le parole
Lo scatto della fronte
sprofonda dentro la mia terra
dentro un progetto di leggero vivere
scrollando temporali
con la pazienza dell'arcobaleno
a curvarsi negli anni
a contemplare i ritorni
noi sbalorditi d'assenza

Si fa più luce
a stupirmi
tocco di corde
a dispiegarsi
piano
piano e forte
mio cielo
in dissolvenza
archi e tempeste
Il silenzio

Pensare alla parola
pensare alla sua cura
goccia che sfugge
sull'orlo della pietra
si dissolve
un po' evaporando
un po' scivolando al di sotto

Ecco la mappa
Il senso
lucente
Da secoli
la cercavo
metafisica
subcoscienza

Era solo metà del cammino
silenzio semiloquace
semimuta parola
fino all'intero
Luce bianca

Ancora attesa
ancora
un'altra notte
L'alba
quando ti raggiungo

AND AS YOU LEAVE THE BAR

And as you leave the bar
you bite into your words
The startle of your brow
collapses inside my clay
inside a project for light living
shaking off thunderstorms
with the patience of the rainbow
curving into the years
gazing at the returns
we, astounded by absence

It's getting brighter
stunning me
like chords playing
unfolding
softly
piano and forte
my sky
dissolving
rainbows and storms
Silence

To think about the word
to think about caring for it
a drop dripping away
on the edge of stone
dissolving
evaporating a little
slipping slightly below

That's the map
Sense
shining
For centuries
I searched for it
metaphysical
subconscience

It was only half way along the path
a semi-loquacious silence
a semi-mute word
until it became whole
White light

Still waiting
still
another night
It will be dawn
when I join you

RAGNO IN GOCCIA D'AMBRA

Se è vero
che la parola vera nasce dal silenzio
voglio tacere. Fino
ad un silenzio compulsivo
Dopo
Dopo lo sperpero dei segni, dopo
la purificazione delle stanze, spenta
l'ultima scintilla sullo schermo
soltanto pietre
da interrogare

Dure. Come irremovibili
speranze. Dure
come disperazioni
Scoprire l'atteggiarsi possibile
della bocca a grido
nel contagio dell'ambra che rafferma
un minimo urlo di Munch

Era
stella viva tra i rami
immobile nel possesso della ragnatela
signore dell'equilibrio nella fragilità
stratega del fulmineo, fulminato
Urlo nel tuo silenzio, taccio
nel tuo grido
ragno in goccia d'ambra

SPIDER IN AN AMBER DROP

If it is true
that the true word is born from silence
I want to be silent. To reach
a compulsive silence
Beyond
Beyond the squandering of signs, beyond
the purification of rooms, when even
the last spark on the screen is out
there will only be stones
to ask questions of

Hard ones. Like stubborn
hopes. As hard
as despair
Discovering the possible setting
of the mouth for shouting
in the contagion of amber that solidifies
a tiny scream by Munch

It was
a living star among the branches
motionless in its dominion of the cobweb
lord of balance amidst fragility
a strategist of lightning, struck by lightning
I scream into your silence, am silent
into your scream
                spider in an amber drop

CANTO DI UNA CONFERMA

Se fosse
pura coincidenza di parametri
a tendere
l'arco innocente della vicenda
Solo un'aria giovane
profumo d'alga iniziale
turbolenza di fango
confuso ancora
tra humus di stelle e tufo di conchiglie

Se fosse
solo biotopos in giusta insolazione
a confermare
la dignità dei vivi
inconsapevoli onde in sinuosa evoluzione

Se fosse
amore solo un'eco parallela
armonia di due eliche abbracciate
a punteggiare
di luci-amplesso il mare
diffusa spuma di desiderio
su questo territorio selvatico di antenne
ubiqua voce:
- Ti ho vista, tu mi hai visto
il tuo ventre si inarca
e mi conosco padre
in questo coraggio largo dispiegato in vela
Mio figlio
sicuro deve adagiarsi
al rito lento della discendenza -

SONG OF CONFIRMATION

What if
purely coincidental parameters
had drawn
the innocent bow of life
Just a youthful breeze
the scent of the first algae
the turbulence of mud
still confused
between the humus of stars and the tufa of shells

What if
just one biotope perfectly sunlit
could confirm
the dignity of the living
in oblivious waves sinuously evolving

What if
love were just a parallel echo
a harmony of two helixes embraced
punctuating
the sea with lights of intercourse
like the diffused foam of desire
over this jungle of antennae
a ubiquitous voice:
- I saw you, you saw me
your belly arches
and I know myself to be a father
sailing fully unfurled into this bravery
My son
must settle confidently
into the slow ritual of lineage -

Se fosse
essere padre
solo orgoglio automatico di geni
- io pronto al mio scarno imprinting -
io, comunque, a insegnargli
l'estrema dignità delle parole

Se fosse
solo squilibrio di parametri
insolente penuria d'acqua o di petrolio
a offuscare
un ragionevole confine
a mescolare
nuovi profili in nuove dimensioni
dialogo offerto del tuo viso ibridato

What if
fatherhood were only
the automatic pride of genes
- me ready for my lean imprinting -
me, in any case, teaching him
the extreme dignity of words

What if
only the imbalance of parameters
the insolent shortage of water or oil
were blurring
peaceful borders
mixing
new profiles with new events
like the dialogue your hybridized face offers

Se fosse
questo vivere imperfetto
puro accidente
anche il tuo stupore
a confermare
la dignità del cerchio accerchiato
Terra
ruota innocente
lungo i nostri sofferti meridiani
madre che mesce vino ingoia sangue
sussulta violata eviscerata
Terra
assopita al canto di nenie circolari
Si leva salda, al sole
perfettamente orientale
a confermare
che attende ogni alba
la sua grande nave

What if
this imperfect way of living
were pure coincidence
even your amazement
confirming
the dignity of the encircled circle
The earth
an innocent wheel
along our suffering meridians
a mother who pours wine swallows blood
is startled raped disembowelled
The earth
soothed by the chant of circular lullabies
rises steadily, towards the sun
perfectly poised in the east
confirming
that she waits at each dawn
for her ship to come in

ORGANISMI GENETICAMENTE MODIFICATI

A perdita d'occhio finalmente chiara
distesa di vergini strade
ad elica, dai nomi
che chiedono d'essere nominati
o solo restare oscuri, se indelicatamente
l'ago scompiglia il nucleo
Gene straniero, ospite
sacro ospite un tempo si onorava
con candidi panni e cibo, mai
si aveva timore
del naufrago alla porta

Ora l'ibridazione mi confondesalta
domino le creature mi domino
come se avessi in dono droga
mosaico di natura snatura
m'innesto ali d'aquila, di certo
un cuore di leone
longevità di tartaruga
Volo
Pluripotente vivo
A lungo sopravvivo

GENETICALLY MODIFIED ORGANISMS

As far as the eye can see, the stretch
of helicoidal virgin roads is finally clear,
with names
begging to be named
or just remain obscure, if the needle
indelicately upsets the nucleus
Foreign gene, guest gene
sacred guest honoured long ago
with pristine robes and food, there was never
any fear
of the shipwrecked man at the door

Now hybridization confusexcites me
I master creatures I master myself
as if I had the gift of drugs
the mosaic of un-natured nature
I graft eagle wings on myself, needless to say
the heart of a lion
the longevity of a tortoise
I fly
I live multi-mightily
A long-term survivor

Non mi riconosco, nuovo
dio della facilità, anche se mi libro
- a mezz'altezza -
anche se ci scambiamo tutti senza fine
geni come figurine
fino ad averle tutte
e poi e poi

Temo me, te temo
perduto il senso
noi d'essere noi
sentire amare noi
sperare

I don't recognize myself as a new
god of ease, even if I soar
- in mid air -
even if all of us endlessly trade genes
amongst ourselves like trading cards
until we have them all
and then and then

I fear me, I fear you
the meaning is lost
of us being us
feeling loving us
hoping

LAMENTO DI FARAONE

Beato ero
bendato
svuotato eppure sazio
imbalsamato
Lasciavo perfino indovinare
un sorriso indulgente
di esatto dio deposto
nel punto di intersezione
dove la geometria del cielo consolava
il pianto notturno delle stelle

Di peso emigrato
spaesato immuseato
assordato
- una babele queste lingue d'oltrafrica -
E poi, mi è proibito dai sacerdoti
ascoltare le vostre risa
dopo l'ultimo pianto
In frantumi
le vibrazioni d'Iside
Capovolto
sul dorso lo scarabeo

A PHARAOH'S LAMENT

Blessed was I
bandaged
emptied yet replete
embalmed
I would even intimate
the indulgent smile
of an exact god deposed
at the point of intersection
where heavenly geometry used to console
the stars' nocturnal wail

Forced to emigrate
Displaced, stuck in a museum
deafened
- these out-of-Africa languages are real babble -
And besides, high priests forbid me
to listen to your laughter
after the last wail
Isis' vibrations
are shattered
The sacred scarab is on its back
upturned

Rendetemi
alla pace tetragona
ombra materna della cuspide
Ho ancora
scorte d'essenza raggrumate
negli occhi nelle narici
Dovevano abbondare
perché non dimenticassi
d'essere figlio d'astri
fin sotto le unghie

Mi squarciaste
la prua del tempo
bozzolo nave in sacra metamorfosi
per scoprire
solo sbuffi di sabbia
(assistevo immobile
io scarabeota)
Sabbia ridatemi sabbia
smeriglio del vento sulle rose
rumore vagabondo delle dune
limo sul pube dell'immensa dea
- sua è la carne dei fiori -

Oh, inonda, Nilo,
terra e cielo tutto
E me
fino alle tue stelle

Take me back
to foursquare peace
the motherly shadow of the cusp
I still have
stores of clotted essence
in my eyes in my nostrils
They had to abound
lest I should forget
I was the son of the stars
even under my fingernails

You ripped open
the prow of time on me
the ship-cocoon in holy metamorphosis
only to discover
gusts of sand
(I watched motionless
like a dumb scarab)
Sand give me back sand
emery blowing on the roses
noise roving over the dunes
silt on the pubes of the boundless goddess
- hers is the flesh of flowers -

O Nile, flood
earth and all the sky
And me, too
up to your stars

ABSURDA

Appena voltato l'angolo non resta
nemmeno l'eco di uno scalpiccìo,
il minimo stupore di un'eclisse *absurdum*

del gran discorrere
solo una velatura scabra
che raschia un po' la gola *absurdum*

Silenzio assordante sulla piazza
assolata di luce catodica
sole catatonico *absurdum*

Ombra rifugio d'ombra scrivere nell'ombra
come sul pavimento di una cattedrale
a decifrare segni nel segreto
consunti per troppo amore
Scrivo in ginocchio
il gemito dei frutti al nascere
il rombo dei rami che sovrastano

ABSURD

Having scarcely turned the corner not even
the echo of shuffling steps remains
the slightest astonishment of an eclipse *absurdum*

after all that talking
there is only a rasping veil
that grates the throat a little *absurdum*

Deafening silence over the square
steeped in cathodic light
catatonic sunshine *absurdum*

Shade a shelter in the shade writing in the shade
as on the floor of a cathedral
deciphering signs in secret
worn from too much love
I write on my knees
about the groan of fruit at birth
the rumble of branches hanging overhead

Se l'ombra di mille cattedrali
mosaico di parole in ombra
agli occhi abbacinati disvelasse
l'ultimo raggio puntiforme *absurdum*
- piume d'angeli
le dita di chi scrive - *absurdum*
un canto sterminato
si ribalterebbe:
tetto del mondo,
luce

Ombra che si fa luce *absurdum*

If the shade of a thousand cathedrals
a mosaic of words in the shade
revealed to our dazzled eyes
the last punctiform ray *absurdum*
- angel feathers
the writer's fingers – *absurdum*
an endless song
would be overturned:
the ceiling of the world,
light

Shade that becomes light *absurdum*

RIBELLIONI

Annuso questo vento
ha l'odore - remoto -
di una stanza umida
odore umido d'infanzia
o forse era solo, nascosta,
una castagna bollita
che si divertiva a marcire

Vento che imbizzarriva gli aquiloni
salivo insieme al vento
per le scale del mondo
coi capelli ribelli
ribelle anche l'anima
agli anni, di onda in onda

Vento bifronte ingannatore
ti ho scoperto
Tu vuoi la tabula rasa, candore
che la furia non merita
Per questo sei condannato alle due facce:
erosione, da un lato
(vita che consumi)
e cumulo, sull'altro versante
(dei rimorsi)

REBELLIONS

I sniff this wind
it smells - remotely -
like a damp room
the damp smell of childhood
or perhaps it was only a boiled
chestnut, hidden,
having fun rotting

Wind that made kites frisky
I would climb together with the wind
up the steps of the world
with my rebellious hair
my spirit rebelling too
over the years, from one wave to another

Two-faced deceitful wind
I'm on to you
You want a tabula rasa, a candour
that fury does not deserve
This is why you are condemned to two faces:
erosion, on one side
(the life you use up)
and accumulation, on the other side
(your regrets)

Oggi ti riconosco il volto caldo
dal sentore orgasmico di sabbia
da quel tuo soffio impollinato d'Africa
Domani sarai profilo boreale
schiaffi di ghiaccio e spine

Il vento gira
Oh gira, vento

Today I recognize your warm face
from the orgasmic whiff of sand
from the pollinated way you blow from Africa
Tomorrow you will be the Boreal profile
ice and thorns slapping my face

The wind whirls
Oh whirl, wind

POLICICLICI IDROCARBURI AROMATICI

E non sapevo di scoprire amici
antichi,
nel sotterraneo andare
aspirando
piccole grida di benzene
tra scie inerti d'azoto
Il poeta sa riconoscere - si dice -
il senso riposto delle cose

Ma queste sono voci
di cellule remote, dissepolte
da mari antichi
animule larvate di petrolio
policiclici idrocarburi aromatici
riconoscibili
dallo spettro di riga
(giungono in riga
le grida degli spettri)

POLYCYCLIC AROMATIC HYDROCARBONS

And I didn't know I was discovering
ancient friends
on my underground travels
sucking up
small cries of benzene
among inert wakes of nitrogen
A poet can tell - they say -
the hidden sense of things

But these are voices
of remote cells, disinterred
from ancient seas
little ghostly petroleum souls
polycyclic aromatic hydrocarbons
detectable
on a line spectrum
(the cries of the spectres
arrive in a line)

Chiedono
la loro antica pace subcrostale
o solo mescolarsi
- polvere nel respiro -
farsi nostro corpo
aderendo perfino
alla suola delle scarpe
compagni, un passo dopo l'altro
al nostro viaggio d'impolverimento

Unirci
tutti questi occhi primordiali
È il mare antico
comune abbraccio nello smarrimento

They ask
for their ancient sub-crustal peace
or simply to mix with us
- dust in each breath -
to become our body
even sticking
to the soles of our shoes
companions, one step after another
on our journey towards dust

What unifies us
primeval eyes all
Is the ancient sea
the mutual embrace when we feel lost

SILENZIO

Attesa di responsi
Farsi lucertola di pietra
al sole. Farsi terra
sulla terra aderendo
distesi
seguendo il naturale disporsi
degli arti - come l'uomo di Leonardo -
lanciati
nelle solenni direzioni
vita-morte
e passato-futuro
(sempre attraversando il cuore)
A lungo
lasciando compiere l'osmosi

Silenzio
Rumore di minimi allungamenti
in questi fili d'erba che il mio corpo preme
dove terra e luce tramano alchimie
Rumore lento di nebbia
che vorrebbe
ottundere quei miseri
miei fuochi residui
affabulando
i suoi racconti stagionali d'acqua

SILENCE

Waiting for answers
Becoming a stone lizard
in the sun. Becoming clay
clinging to the ground
                    stretched out
following the natural arrangement
of the limbs - like Leonardo's man -
                                        splayed
in the solemn directions
life-death
and past-future
(always going through the heart)
                                        All along
letting osmosis run its course

Silence
The sound of minimal growth
from these blades of grass that my body flattens
where clay and light plot alchemies
The slow sound of fog
that would wish
to put out those wretched
residual fires of mine
                         spinning a yarn
out of its seasonal tales of water

Silenzio
Attesa di fusione
O d'altro arcano, visto
che già siamo
ombra terraquea
Fino al prorompere dell'alba

Silence
Waiting for fusion
Or for another mystery, seeing
as we are already
a claywatery shadow
Until dawn breaks

NOMI PER UN'ISOLA

Non chiamatemi isola
Chiamatemi *quiete inquieta*
a pochi passi dal rogo
dove la cadenza di luce
ha pure lacrime
Chiamatemi *terra di nascite*
desiderio di tregua
illimite speranza tra le spine
Chiamatemi *vista sul cielo*
ipnotica
occhio d'oliva
castano contro azzurro
a notte ubriaco di stelle
di grida

Non chiamatemi isola
Chiamatemi *nodo di rete*
dove s'impiglia il poeta
a rubare bellezza al buio
Questo mare di rose
rosmarino
ape febbrile ronza
di spruzzi alle finestre
Questo mare timo-re
sovrano che s'infoglia
al centro del mio abbandono
Chiamatemi *seme di mare sull'abisso*
Da ingenui arrembaggi mi salva
una muta di mandorli e delfini
(il tempo non ha che lame di schiuma)

NAMES FOR AN ISLAND

Do not call me island
Call me *restless rest*
a few paces from the pyre
where the lilting light
sheds pure tears
Call me *land of births*
desire for truce
boundless hope through the thorns
Call me *hypnotic*
                    view of the sky
olive eye
brown against blue
drunk at night on stars
                              on shouts

Do not call me island
Call me *knot in a net*
where the poet gets enmeshed
stealing beauty from the darkness
This rosemary sea
                    of marine roses
a feverish bee buzzes
sea-spray on windows
This mari-thyme sha-king
a sovereign sprouting leaves
at the centre of my abandonment
Call me *sea seed on the abyss*
I am saved from naive boardings
by a team of almonds and dolphins
(time only has foam blades)

Chiamatemi *messaggio pietrificato*
bottiglia dei giganti di Pasqua
tangente d'amore attraverso l'oceano
magmatico canto sotterraneo

Non chiamatemi isola
Chiamatemi *schianto d'un ricordo*
casa ritrovata, corrosa, ma salva dall'oblio
tana larvale
riposo su pietre levigate, mai vinte
Chiamatemi *favola in sogno*
quindi *doppio sogno*
trama del tempo, dove
il destino fiorisce nella grande
domanda della notte

Non so se inganno o ritrosia
questo accerchiarmi d'onde di speranza
E poi lasciarmi
ad asciugare il diluvio
Della mappa del pianto
solo un'orma di saudade
Così insegno
la geografia del limite
                                        e a varcarlo
Ci sarà sempre un'isola
aspra, guado di rabbia e festa
                                        alle parole

Call me *message turned to stone*
a bottle from the Easter giants
love's tangent across the ocean
magmatic subterranean song

Do not call me island
Call me *crashing memory*
recovered house, corroded, but saved from oblivion
a lair for larva
repose on smooth, unvanquished stones
Call me *fairytale in a dream*
therefore *double dream*
time's plot, where
fate flowers in the great
question of the night

I don't know whether this girdling myself
with waves of hope is deceit or coyness
Leaving me later
to dry out the flood
From the map of tears
there's only a trace of saudade
This is how I teach
the geography of limit
                                        to cross it
there will always be a rugged
island, a ford of rage and feasts
                                        leading to words

UN VIAGGIO UN SOLE UNA LUNA

Lucidi calzari di una notte lucida
fuori dal tempo, sulla soglia, fermi
Pietrificati atleti in attesa
del segnale
- stanotte qualche rivolo di luce si prevede
dai calici del cielo -
Appena cade la mia stella, scattano

Esagerato slancio, mie scarpette
per una gara
che è solo minima maratona
una salita di convolvolo
Dalla radice alla gemma apicale
si viaggia in vortice,
dilatando l'ascolto in foglie alterne

Dirige il sole: massima orchestra,
minime variazioni. Regolari
scrosci di clorofilla nei tornanti
come fiotti nel cuore, inesorabile
respiro regolare della vita
Il sole insiste sul vibrato termico
Sole drummer drammatico (sole batterista)
Sole alchimista incendiario
Sole cenere
Sole nube-avaro
Sole eclisse
Sole di solitudini
Sole binging (ingordo)
Avvizzisce-divora, a ogni giro, una campanula
(a sera lo stormo blu tintinna nella gola)

A VOYAGE A SUN A MOON

Shiny shoes for a shiny night
beyond time, on the threshold, motionless
Petrified athletes waiting
for the signal
- tonight the odd trickle of light is expected
from the goblets in the sky -
Scarcely has my star fallen, than my pumps

jump up in an exaggerated leap
for a race
that's only a minor marathon
a climb up bindweed
From the root to the bud at the top
we travel in a vortex
dilating our hearing in alternate leaves

The sun is conducting: full orchestra,
minor variations. Regular
storms of chlorophyll at the sharp bends
like floods in our heart, the inexorable
regular breath of life
The sun insists on thermal vibrato
Sun as dramatic drummer
Sun as incendiary alchemist
Sun as ashes
Sun as cloud-begrudger
Sun as eclipse
Sun as solitude
Sun as greedy binges
It withers-devours, at every turn, a bellflower
(at night the blue flock rings in its throat)

Notte di brina sulle gemme, ghiaccio
sulla cima del mondo
Irrigiditi calzari alla deriva. Arranco
perdo la memoria dei soli
e la muta di cani ed angeli
è muta. Scivolo
sulla slitta di Amundsen, carica di stelle

Sulla cima del mondo
coi calzari fradici
cancello le mie tracce, ma non posso
nascondermi alla luna

Night of frost on the buds, ice
on top of the world
Stiff snow-boots, drifting. I am hobbling
losing my memory of the suns
and the team of dogs and angels
is mute. I am sliding
on Amundsen's sled, laden with stars

On top of the world
with drenched shoes
I erase my tracks, but I cannot
hide from the moon

da

CURVE DI LIVELLO

(2006)

from

CONTOUR LINES

(2006)

ANCORA SIANO I SEGNI

Ancora siano i segni sulle rocce
a dischiudere il tempo
profili di guerrieri e bisonti
in corsa, sotto un piccolo sole
in forma di stella

ansanti
per chilometri brillanti di pioggia
profili di automobilisti e tir
sommersi da onde radio

vibra
un dolmen poco lontano
con forza immobile
convoca mani e rami
Tre pietre
- minima famiglia sfuggita al diluvio -
in silenzio guardarle nella notte
accostando l'orecchio al tronco dell'ulivo
sentirsi roccia linfa voce
arca approdata e fusa in terra

Ancora siano i segni sulle pagine
a traghettare il tempo: lontanissimi
lembi di cielo pulsanti sulle onde
inondano lo schermo, si raggiungono

MAY THE SIGNS CONTINUE

May the signs on the rocks
continue to unveil time
the profiles of warriors and bison
are running under a tiny sun
the shape of a star

panting
for rain-dazzled kilometres
the profiles of drivers and trucks
submerged in radio waves

not far away
a dolmen vibrates
with stillness of strength
calling for hands and branches
Three stones
- the smallest family saved from the flood -
you could watch them in silence at night
with your ear against the olive tree trunk
feel you are rock lymph voice
the ark docked and fused to the ground

May the signs on the pages
continue to ferry time: far away
strips of sky beating on the waves
flood the screen, join together

Dammi parole dunque, e segni
piangi sulla mia spalla, o ridi
offrimi le scene della gioia
incontrami

prima che si diradi la foresta
prima che accada il nero errore
prima dell'ultima risata
(la ruota della terra
è il suo continuo ridere, convulso)

Give me words, so, and signs
cry on my shoulder, or laugh
offer me joyful scenes
find me

before the forest is thinned out
before the darkness of error falls
before the last laugh
(the earth's rotation
is its own continuous laugh, cracking up)

MEDITERRANEO

Marina Serra. Assalto
di un'alba nitida, capace
di spingere i monti d'Albania
fin qui, sotto il balcone
Posso toccarli quasi
fianchi verdi e radici
intrecciate alle mie
Da costa a costa
scintillano di senso le correnti
lu rusciu de lu mare
canta in mediterraneo

Potevo essere nata su quei monti
e mia madre avermi lavata nel canale d'Otranto
nutrita con zuppa d'alghe e filastrocche di Lushnje
potevo trovarmi in quella barca
così traboccante di speranza
che i fianchi non reggevano al rimorso

Mi trovo in quella barca, sono
albanese, pure
messapicagrecaegizialibica
il mio sangue è incontro d'onde
paziente e antico
(continua a mescolare
questo inascoltato mare)

MEDITERRANEAN

Marina Serra. The assault
of a bright dawn, capable
of pushing the mountains of Albania
to here, under the balcony
I can almost touch them
green slopes and roots
intertwined with mine
From coast to coast
tides gleam with meaning
the rush of the sea
sings in Mediterranean

I could have been born on those mountains
bathed by my mother in the Otranto canal
reared on algae soup and rhymes from Lushnje
I could have found myself on that boat
overflowing with so much hope
its sides couldn't handle the remorse

I am on that boat, I am
Albanian
greekmessapicegyptianlybian too
my blood is the patient, age-old
confluence of waves
(constantly churning
this unheeded sea)

SULL'OTTAVA ELEGIA DI RILKE

La casa ha finestre sul mare
per ricordare l'origine
il vortice la calma le vele millenarie
i ritorni che volgono in commiati
partenze per altri oceani

Il giardino ha pini d'aleppo e olivi
per ospitare chi non sa della morte:
insetti e uccelli, volpi
notturne, a volte - immobili-
guardano anch'esse il mare
come per un abbaglio misterioso
- gli animali mai fissano
la morte negli occhi -
noi l'abbiamo a fianco e miopi
vediamo il cielo accendersi di fuochi
e i luoghi dove
lei ciecamente piove

La rosa veloce sfoglia
in silenzio le spine si preparano
a penetrarci le carni
il mare a sommergere il disordine
gli abbracci misti a spari nonostante
l'angoscia suonata a stormo
dalle cicale sui rami

Dai pini volano
rondini al sud, imperturbate

AFTER RILKE'S EIGHTH ELEGY

The house has windows to the ocean
so as to recall the beginning
the ancient vortex, calm, millennial sails
returns that turn to farewells
odysseys bound for other seas

In the garden aleppo pines and olive trees
welcome those who know nothing of death:
insects and birds, sometimes
nocturnal foxes - motionless -
also look out to sea
as if mysteriously dazzled
- animals never look
death in the eye -
we live with it by our side, shortsighted
see the sky light up with flames
and the places where
death blindly rains

The rose soon loses its leaves
in silence its thorns make ready
to pierce our flesh
the sea to submerge disorder
hugs are mixed with gunshots despite
the unease of cicadas
swarming in the trees

From the pines, swallows fly
south, undaunted

PIAZZA JEMAA EL FNA

Entro in Jemaa el Fna
quasi cadendo sul fango secco
rinnovando il parto
del feto antico di me africana
Le narici inalano magia di terra
mentaradiciossaconsunte
Già sortilegio è l'amnesia
della tribù bianca lontana
sterilizzata, muta

La piazza ha occhi che saettano
arcaiche voci acute, per udirsi nel vento
storie mimate come graffiti
Sono io quella che percuote il timpano
batte i piedi curva sul ritmo
assorbe l'ipnosi del serpente
che si solleva molle, stanco di ripetersi
mi guarda, incredibilmente amico

E strana pure questa voglia di datteri
oltre il sapore, smania
che l'oro bruno penetri la pelle
(forse i geni mutano così
sotto il sole, per amore-mimesi
di naturadonosopravvivenza)

JEMAA EL FNA SQUARE

I enter Jemaa el Fna
almost stumbling on dry earth
re-enacting the delivery
of an ancient foetus, my African self
My nostrils inhaling earth magic
made of mintrootswornbones
The amnesia of the distant
white tribe, sterilized and mute
is already sorcery

The square has eyes that pierce like arrows
archaic voices sharp enough to carry on the wind
mimed stories like graffiti
I am the one who beats the drum
stomps her feet flows to the rhythm
absorbs the hypnosis of the snake
as it rises, supple, tired of repetition
staring at me, unbelievably friendly

And it's strange, this urge for dates
beyond their taste, a craving
for bronzed gold to penetrate my skin
(maybe this is how genes mutate
under the sun, out of mimetic love
of naturegiftsurvival)

Continentale perdono d'Africa
nei visi offerti insieme ai piccoli oggettintarsio
di orgogliosperanzasudore
(s'addensa ovunque il sudore
impastato nel fango, edificato nelle case)
Così da sempre la terra si fa umana

Sento le rughe della madre, vive

Continental forgiveness on the African faces
offered with little objects inlaid
with pridehopesweat
(the sweat condensing everywhere
kneaded in the mud, built into houses)
That's always been how the earth becomes human

I feel the mother's wrinkles, alive

FORSE CON UNA DONNA

Lasciarla far luce
con le sue lanterne, vigile
sulle alte mura trasparenti
lasciarla apparire e sparire
come lei vuole
dosare i richiami
perché possa appartarsi
in qualche sua giungla di luna

Forse con una donna
disperata di te, del tuo mondo
non serve dividere corone
meglio farsi esuli insieme
navigare con lei navicella lunare
approdare su placide ginecosfere
dove lei è dispensiera
di pane e parole

Forse con una donna
sentire più spesso stupore
che istupidimento, soprattutto
quando dalle macerie risorgono
lentamente i villaggi
illimpiditi dal pianto e lei
ricomincia a parlare alle rose

MAYBE WITH A WOMAN

Let her shine a light
with her lanterns, watch
over the high transparent walls
let her appear and disappear
as she wishes
negociate the demands
so she can slip away
into one of her lunar jungles

Maybe sharing a crown with a woman
troubled by you, by your world
is useless
best become exiles together
sail her like a little moon boat
berth in placid gynaecospheres
where she dispenses
bread and words

Maybe with a woman
you could more often feel wonder
instead of being stunned, especially
when the debris slowly
reemerges as towns
cleansed by the wailing and she
starts talking to the roses again

Forse con una donna
ridere insieme
della tua enfasi e imperfezione
lei complice custode
di pienezza e inquietudine
del riso e del pathos
che non debordi
nel suo patimento

Ti immerge
nella morbida offerta
tu colmo di lei le correnti
inverti al tuo mare, dissenti
dal banditore che eri
(ora più aperte sul mondo le porte)

Maybe with a woman
you could laugh together
about your bravado and imperfection
she, your accomplice, custodian
of satisfaction and unease
of the laughter and pathos
you won't spill
on her suffering

She immerses you
in her tender offer
you, overflowing with her, change the course
of the currents in your sea, giving up
the town crier that you were
(the doors to the world more open now)

EVA
(diario dall'Eden)

Alba. Mi sveglia
un'inquietudine lucida: solito
letto di fiori, solito
traboccante profumo
Nausea. Questa luce imperiosa
che mi ama in ogni millimetro, eterna
Mi vedo deforme
in questa veste deiforme, perfetta

Ho sognato, stanotte
profezie di dolore: vagavo
lupa in cattività, nel Giardino
sontuoso, immutabile
Non resisto. Allo zenit fuggo
decisa, sotto l'ombra del melo

Scelgo. Il dolore che libera
la finitezza del tempo
Addento
la polpa sapida e bassa
che mi abbassa
fino alla terra scarlatta, all'essenza
dell'humus, sangue della nascita

EVE
(Eden diary)

Dawn. I am woken
by a bright unease: the same old
bed of flowers, the same old
overflowing perfume
Nausea. This imperious light
loving every inch of me, is eternal
I feel deformed
in this godly uniform, perfect

Last night I dreamt
about prophecies of pain: I was wandering
like a wolf in captivity, in the luscious
Garden, immutable
I can't take it. At the zenith I flee
determined, under the shade of the apple tree

I choose. The pain that frees
the finiteness of time
I sink my teeth
into the delicious lowly pith
that brings me low
down to red earth, to the essence
of humus, the blood of birth

Notte. Adamo
oh mio capitano
non puoi che seguirmi
seguire il vaso intuitivo
di femmina, il tuo femminile
cavità del tuo desiderio
pienezza della mia costruzione

Benedico quel frutto
E' valso soffrire se il grido
mentre offro mio figlio alla terra
il mio grido, il suo grido
è sublime

Germogliano intanto
i semi di mela che avevo sputato
Intorno
        ho un ardente meleto

Nightfall. Adam
oh my captain
you can only follow me
follow the intuitive vessel
of womanhood, your own femininity
the cavity of your desire
the fullness of my formation

I bless that fruit
It's worth suffering if the cry
while I offer my son to the earth
my cry, his cry
is sublime

Meanwhile, the apple pips
I had spat out are sprouting
Around me
            I have an ardent orchard

NOTTE TARANTA

Anche se quell'aia è lontana
e l'eco dei tamburelli si perde
resta un'essenza ritmica di grano
l'impronta danzante di una mano

Anche se tutto il male di stelle
che doveva piovere è piovuto
la notte regala ancora lumi
fuochi fatui di timpani che ondeggiano
ancora note sul ciglio della morte
fiati sul collo della serpe
passi che sollevano ondate
sospingono il buio nella rete

Si sale inconsapevoli su fili
tesi tra terra e luna
già l'eco fossile canta
allo spazio la rivincita sul ragno
il pane ha battuto il ferro
il sangue rientrato in vena

In alto il nostro suono indelebile
oscilla quantica
l'offerta di una mano

NIGHT OF THE TARANTA

Even with the barnyard far away
and the echo of tambourines fading
there remains a rhythmic essence of wheat
the dancing imprint of a hand

Even when all the evils of the stars
that should have rained down, have rained
the night still offers light
will-o'-the-wisps like drums, undulating
notes still lingering around death
breaths on the serpent's neck
steps that churn up waves
propel the night into the net

We rise unsuspecting along threads
tensed between earth and moon
the fossil echo in space is already singing
a renewed victory over the spider
bread has defeated iron
blood has re-entered the veins

High up, our indelible sound
in a quantum move
a helping hand is offered

CURVE DI LIVELLO

Sebbene la mia carta sia disposta
col margine superiore volto a nord
non ritrovo né oriente né occidente
La carta sembra ormai dis-orientata

Nulla, della fissità cartografica, tranne
un'attitudine incerta, tremula
resistenza alla deriva
Ondeggiano le isoipse - eppure sono sobria -
scosse, come su di una faglia in atto
si slacciano i punti dalle linee
non più obbedienti all'ordine
- tutti in riga, allo stesso livello sul mare -

Una nuova linea si ricompone, lucida
s'allunga, veloce
saetta sulla carta, la perfora
transfuga scia di luce vola
sul nostro cerchio, lieve
ci tocca in fronte, in petto

Allineati, ci stringiamo le mani
bruciamo di limpida invasione
Fugge, caricata di luce, pellegrina
dei continenti. Si ricercano
punti - allo stesso - livello - d'amore

CONTOUR LINES

Despite my map being laid out
with the upper edge facing North
I can find neither East nor West
By now the map seems dis-orientated

Not a trace of cartographic fixity except
for an uncertain ability, a quivering
resistance to being adrift
The contour lines wobble - even though I'm sober-
shaken, as if on an active fault
Points unfasten from the lines
no longer obeying order
- all in a row, at the same level over the sea -

A new line is drawn, brightly
stretches, swift
as an arrow on paper, piercing it
like a fugitive wake of light it flies
over our circle, softly
touches our brow, our breast

We hold hands in a row
burning with joy at the invasion
The line flees, laden with light, a pilgrim
of the continents. The search goes on
for points - on the same - level - as love

KAMIKAZE

Ora la notte è muta

Nell'attimo della tua scissione, nel riverbero
del rito appena consumato
udisti i venti di dio affievolirsi
i cieli chiedere solo nubi

- Estremo flashback - ti vedesti
bambino, tra mille e un fratello
porti - sempre la stessa -
domanda muta, udire
mille e una risposta
chiare, dai burka trasparenti
di mille e una madre

Seguivi il filo inconfondibile
che lega al possibile
mille e una parola
Poiché solo le parole deflagrano
abbattono muri, in cascata
crollano altri muri, avanzano
nuove ere
al passo di mille e una fiaba, vere

KAMIKAZE

The night is now mute

The moment you ripped open, in the reverberation
of the ritual just performed
you heard the winds of god weaken
the skies ask only for clouds

- Final flashback - you saw yourself
as a child, among a thousand and one brothers
asking the same mute question
- over and over - hearing
a thousand and one clear replies
from the transparent burkas
of a thousand and one mothers

You were following the unmistakable thread
that connects to possibility
a thousand and one words
Because only words can blow up
tear down walls, other walls
crumble in cascades, new eras
advance at the pace
of a thousand and one true tales

Eri un uomo rivoluzionato, fatto
d'erba e d'ali, di sangue, fatto
d'ogni conosciuto sangue
ibrido plurimescolato
bastardo benedetto
unica condizione necessaria
per scivolare insieme
fino alla radura sonora
dove inermi
interroghiamo la notte

You were a man renewed from the inside out
made of grass and wings, blood, a man
with every known blood type
a multi-fused hybrid,
a marvellous mongrel
the only condition required
to amble together
as far as the resonant clearing
where defenseless
we question the night

MARIA DEL VENERDI SANTO

Per toni bassi, Maria, posso
ascoltarti, nonostante
le drammatiche pieghe nella veste
il tuo lutto negli occhi

Sorella di ogni mia sorella in pianto
ondeggi, portata a spalla
da uomini in dubbio
per campi minati desertificati

Tornerai dietro i fiori di carta
nella nicchia all'incrocio
di vie che divergono
immobile a piangere
un cielo intero di madre
Intorno ancora puttane
poche madriterese
e la furia del vento la gara
di uomini e foglie - in corsa
s'impolverano e sono già polvere -

Siamo terra che trascolora, Maria
antiche pitture colpite dall'aria
sublimi dileguano
il tuo viola-tragico
il mio bruno-blasfemo

Fluttuano fuse confuse
in cosmico amore molecole
di vesti di croci di foglie

MARY ON GOOD FRIDAY

In hushed tones, Mary,
I can hear you, despite
the dramatic folds of your gown
the mourning in your eyes

Sister to all my wailing sisters
you loll, carried on the shoulders
of doubting men
through deserted minefields

You'll go back behind the paper flowers
on the shrine at the crossroads
where paths diverge
and stand motionless, weeping
an entire sky of mothers
All around there are whores
few motherteresas
and the fury of the wind the race
of men and leaves - as they run
they fall in the dust and are already dust -

Mary, we are earth changing colour
like old paintings subjected to air
your tragic-mauve
my blasphemous-brown
fading

Fluttering in the confusion a fusion
of cosmic molecular love
gowns crosses leaves

OGGI UNA DONNA

Dall'alto riunisce le colline
regina delle voci
colma le valli di nuova terra
accende nuovi fuochi meticci
da cui la foresta rinasce innocente

Indossa la bianca veste
d'Antigone disobbediente
scrive per dire no
alla morte per-uomo
scrive per chiedere

Vulnerabile e potente
col passo di luna destinata
ricomincia da zero-ground, dovunque
ritorna a sollevare l'anfora
- chissà un giro di parole disseta -
scrive per chiedere
per intimare al tempo di rispondere

TODAY A WOMAN

From above, the queen of voices
reunites the hills
fills the valleys with new earth
lights new hybrid fires
from which the forest is reborn, innocent

She wears disobedient Antigone's
white robe
she writes to say no
to death inflicted by man
she writes to plead

Vulnerable and strong
at a pace the moon decrees
she begins again from ground zero, wherever
she is she returns to lift the amphora
- maybe a round of words can quench thirst -
she writes to plead
insisting that time respond

NEMMENO FOSSI AD ALCATRAZ

segregata - è in Roma babelica
che vivo, immersa nella calca -
mai avrei pensato di dipendere
così dalle parole, più da quelle
incorporee, che arrivano
improvvise al telefono, così dense
che intravedo lo sguardo
di chi parla scrutarmi ad ogni sillaba

poi da quelle
che piombano sul monitor
fibrillandomi in petto
aperto un sipario di terra assolata
- i pochi angoli d'ombra, in tumulto -

Spiarne i dettagli è sopravvivere
allo stupore dell'origine
come in estate festeggiare il raccolto
sull'aia antica - il cielo aveva lampi -

E' qui che si nasconde l'angelo
quel che mi resta di anima

YOU'D THINK I WAS IN ALCATRAZ

segregated - though I live in the babel of Rome
immersed in crowds -
I'd never have expected to depend
on words like this, mostly on those
disembodied ones that come
unexpectedly over the phone, so intense
I can make out the speaker's gaze
scrutinizing my every syllable

then on those
that tumble into the monitor
fibrillating my heart
a curtain opening on to sun-drenched earth
- the few corners of shade, in turmoil -

Spying the details is how to survive
the wonder of the beginning
like when we'd celebrate the summer harvest
at the old farmyard - the sky lit by lightning -

This is where angels are hiding
where you'll find what's left of my spirit

BLACKROCK

E' qui, da qualche parte
una sibilla ignota, celtica
Il tocco della veste
dove l'onda s'increspa
il suo respiro, dove una piuma
mulinella   l'acqua
le vive moltitudini vibranti
la vocecanto di sorgente   l'acqua
racconta l'attrazione sacra
l'ingresso nella festa dei corpi   l'acqua
accompagna la dissoluzione
piano, fino alla foce   d'acqua
responso sulle foglie: chiara
la terra capovolta, riflesso il cielo

E noi, sul fondo, solo
memoria di parole

BLACKROCK

She's here, somewhere
an unkown Celtic sybil
The brush of her gown
where a wave ripples
her breath, where a feather
swirls   water
its vibrant swarms are alive
its voicesong from the spring   water
telling of sacred attraction
entry to the feast of bodies   water
bringing slow decay
to the rivermouth   a watery
response on leaves: clear
earth, up-ended, the sky reflected

And we, at the bottom,
are but the memory of words

DIALOGO

fermati, non svanire	
sono stanca	*sono qui*
di braccarti, sperare	
di snidarti	*mi hai sfiorato*
lacerare i tuoi veli	
inflessibili	*già non sono più qui*
da sempre so che ami	
nasconderti	*correre*
ma non del tutto	*per labirinti*
ti piace	
lasciare qualche traccia	*glissare*
negli angoli più impensati	*per circonvoluzioni*
lembo di veste, aroma	
squarcio d'ombra	
da te piovono segni	*tutto è già scritto*
sillabe	*tutto è già detto*
flebili come finale d'eco	
roco rimprovero	
singhiozzo	*tutto è già ascoltato*

DIALOGUE

stop, don't disappear
I'm tired
I'm here
of hunting you, hoping
to flush you out
you've grazed me
rip up your rigid
veils
I'm not here any more

I know you've always loved
hiding
running
though not completely
through mazes
you like
leaving some trace
sliding
in the most unexpected corners
through convolutions
the hem of a gown, a scent
the tear in a shadow

signs shower down from you
everything has already
been written

syllables
everything has already
been said

faint like the tail end of an echo
a raucous reproach
a sob
everything has already
been heard

queste mura	
sono ormai diroccate	
ma scavo ancora	*e ancora non mi vedi*
per nuove fondamenta	
dovunque, soprattutto	*guarda*
dove il terreno frana	*dove la terra freme*
difficile spianare	
un largo spazio acustico	
perché si avverta	
almeno il tuo respiro	*è sui ponti che soffio*
difficile abbattere	
ogni altro muro	*là trattengo il respiro*
mi riduco	
a sottrarti il pane quotidiano	
tenendo tutto a mente	*sono per labirinti, ancora*
scrivo per giorni niente	
sperando che capitoli	
per fame	*sei tu l'affamata*
un giorno	
ti toglierò anche l'acqua	*sei tu l'assetata*
prosciugherò l'oceano	
dove nuoti in silenzio	*negli abissi il silenzio è fragore*
frammenti curvi	*domande, sì*
raccoglierò sul fondo	
simili a riccioli	
di bambino	*nascere, rinascere*

these walls
are now in ruins
but I keep digging *and you still can't see me*
for new foundations
anywhere, especially *look*
where the land is subsiding *where the earth is trembling*

it's hard to level off
a long acoustic space
so your breath at least
will be noticed *the bridges are where I blow*
it's hard to pull down
every other wall *that's where I hold my breath*

I'm reduced
to taking your daily bread from you
keeping everything in mind *I'm still wandering*
through mazes

for days I write nothing
waiting for you to capitulate
from hunger *you're the one who's starving*
one day
I'll deprive you of water too *you're the one who's parched*
I'll dry up the ocean
where you swim in silence *silence screams in*
each abyss

at the bottom I'll collect *questions, yes*
curved fragments
similar to a child's
curls *being born, reborn*

alludi *mi illudo*
alla vita che rifiorisce *forse*
sul ciglio di ogni pozzo
e si ubriaca di canto *vivere è canto*

mille corone ho intrecciato *la vanità*
mille lune ho acceso *sempre oscura la scena*
mille parole a darti corpo *prova, riprova*
ormai non temo
di incontrare il tuo sguardo *coraggio!*
svelati *impossibile*
o dileguati *assurdo*

you allude *I delude myself*
to the life that blossoms again *perhaps*
on the edge of every well
getting drunk on song *song is life*

I've interwoven a thousand crowns *vanity*
lit a thousand moons *always darkens the scene*
a thousand words to shape you *try, try again*
I'm not afraid any more
of meeting your gaze *you can do it!*
show yourself *impossible*
or disappear *absurd*

SU DISCO

L'intercalare semplice
dei giorni delle notti
la folgorante replica
la ruota dell'evento
è stordimento, poi
non puoi dire che tutto questo
incattivisce, costringe alla rovina
a chiudersi in un tank. Semmai trascina
a ruotare, semplicemente
con barbaglio intermittente:
luce negli incontri / ombra
nelle domande antiche
E' tutto. Null'altro da cui derivi
fatale la devastazione
Giochiamo il gioco semplice
del lasciare o prendere:
lasciare
spegnersi in gola il canto
il seme farsi estraneo alla terra
smarrirsi i geni nelle macchine
o prendere
il primo nodo dell'abbraccio
come lasciapassare
emblema quotidiano da esibire
al mattino e ottenere
il diritto alla notte

Su disco lasciare ancora, graffite
le nostre figure in cerchio, sbigottite
il sole scuro, il fungo
l'incerta aurora

ON DISC

The simple interweaving
of days into nights
the dazzling repetition
the wheel of the event
are dizzying, you can't
then say all this
makes us bad, forces us to destroy
shut ourselves inside a tank. Rather,
it forces us to rotate, simply
with an intermittent spark:
light in our encounters / shade
in old questions
That's all. Nothing else contributes
to our fatal destruction
We play a simple game
of taking or leaving:
leaving
the song in our throat die out
the seed grow alien to the earth
genes lose their way in machines
or taking
the first squeeze of a hug
like a pass
some daily symbol we can show
in the morning that might gain us
the right to make it to night

Leaving on disc once again, the record
of our faces in a circle, shocked
the blackened sun, mushroom clouds
the uncertain dawn

PLANISFERI

Mi sta stretta la planitudine
la contentezza dell'orizzonte
la sua sazia piega
di racconto finito
erosione compiuta
Preferisco i versanti inquieti
il moto ondulante
dei desideri delle profezie
la statua barcollante
portata a spalla in processione

La superficie piatta dell'oceano
può solo incresparsi, inebetita
dalla misura. Ma in basso
i fondali covano
voglia ribelle di corrugarsi
ergersi, unirsi
tanto, da farsi male
(forse solo dall'insensatezza
è fatale rinascere)

Così l'occhio del dolore
è l'occhio delle guglie
l'occhio della città
l'invito al respiro
lo spigolo che taglia la verità
soffia via la sabbia
sospende le leggi di gravità

PLANISPHERES

Flatness constrains me
the happiness of the horizon
its bend smug
as the end of a story
the erosion complete
I prefer unsettled slopes
the undulating motion
of hopes and prophecies
the wavering statue
shouldered in a procession

The flat surface of the ocean
can only ripple, numbed
by its scale. But below
the sea bed is brooding
with a rebellious urge to ridge
rise, collide
hard, enough to get hurt
(maybe rebirth only comes
from folly)

Thus the eye of pain
is the eye of the summits
the eye of the city
the invitation to breathe
the edge that carves out truth
blows away sand
suspends the laws of gravity

da

POESIE INEDITE

(2007-2009)

from
UNPUBLISHED POEMS
(2007-2009)

EVOLUZIONE DI UNA PERFORMANCE

vorrei dir**vi** -no- piuttosto dir**ti**
la mia poesia, vorrei
da te ascolto lancinante
risposta acuminata
come fossimo solo noi due
con l'oceano nel mezzo
e ti stessi scrivendo
la mia lettera estrema, di consegna

così non mi esibisco
m'invento una parabola
più o meno acuta
più o meno musicale
per chiederti una maglia
alla rete da lanciare
noi tutti in mare

se solo qui e subito ognuno
salendo sul mio palco
dell'incertezza
mi rispondesse muto
- in mano la sua lettera -
sarei il più raggiante dei vincitori
in questo silenzio
che ci esplode in segni

EVOLUTION OF A PERFORMANCE

I don't want to tell all of you my poem
just you, I'd like
piercing attention from you
a sharpened response
as if there were just the two of us
with the ocean in between
and I were writing you
my last letter

that way I can't show off
I invent a parable
more or less clever
more or less musical
to ask you for some mesh
for the net we will all cast
out to sea

if only here, and now, everyone
climbed onto the stage
of my uncertainty
and gave me a mute reply
- holding my letter in their hand -
I'd be the most radiant of victors
in this silence
exploding into signs around us

EXTRANEE STRUTTURE

sul monitor sei
senza tregua né appigli
guardo le tue pupille mai sazie
di lumi extranei
sulla tua fronte inquieta piove
un'insidia di voci tenuissime
dall'accesa coppa virtuale

hai sulla testa
non un antiquato, di certo, serto di lauro
ma una lucida tecnocorona
barbara, sfolgorante. La mente
- che non ha chiesto protesi -
                                        vacilla

XTRANGE STRUCTURES

you're at the monitor
with no truce or hold
I look at your pupils never sated
by xtrange lights
a snare of very faint voices
rains on your anxious brow
from the vivid virtual cup

on your head you sport
not an ancient laurel wreath, of course
but a bright technocrown
barbarous, dazzling. The mind
- not having asked for a prosthesis -
boggles

BIONANOSTRUTTURE

avrò anch'io, come il geco nelle zampette
in qualche area inesplorata del cervello del cuore
sterminati minimi bioappigli
                                        angstrom
capaci di sorreggere
il tuo peso sfrontato di bastione

ti sostengo
urtando urlando contro il cielo
mio masso di Stonehenge
col tatuaggio del nome tuo ripetuto
in finissime impronte
- come sulla foglia di loto -
                    sul mio petto

BIONANOSTRUCTURES

maybe, like the gecko's little legs
some unexplored part of my brain or my heart
also has tiny infinite angstrom
                                        bioholds
capable of bearing
your shameless bulwark weight

I hold you up
my Stonehenge boulder
pounding shouting at the sky
your name repeatedly tattooed
in gossamer impressions
- as on a lotus leaf -
                              on my chest

GRANDI MADRI DI MALTA

equivalenza dell'aspetto fertile del tempo
a questa madre
feliceobesa guardiana di Tarxien
curvilinea di abbracci

semplicità del corpo senza necessità di scrittura
parola sazia sacrale
indicando la direzione morbida innocente

doni di granomiele e seme
inarcano i fianchi
il ventretempio imita il cielo
le nove lune trascorrono
in sonno largo di incontri

madre dormiente in preascolto del vagito, pure
del nostro lamento

GREAT MOTHERS OF MALTA

the fertile aspect of time
is equivalent to this mother
a happyobese guardian of Tarxien
curvilinear with hugs

the simplicity of her body needs no writing
like the sated sacred word
pointing out the soft innocent path

gifts of honeywheat and seed
curve her thighs
her wombtemple imitates the sky
the nine moons go by
in a long slumber of encounters

sleeping mother wakeful to the newborn's cry, even
to our lament

UN'ARIA DI FORESTA MI BATTE SULLE GUANCE

un'aria di foresta mi batte sulle guance
sto volando
a braccia distese esploro un sogno
siamo voci in stormo
come in cammino su un sentiero d'aria
con la conchiglia la veste monacale
          la sera irradia pulsazioni di canto

sto scrivendo
della mia stanza dell'incertezza
nel bagliore tenue dello schermo
che sottrae voce, *emoticons*
a surrogare parole-carezze sulla pelle   pelle
che almeno scorticasse
della superbia della competizione
della frazione ormai plasmatica del male
oh quanti siamo in astinenza
e la dose d'amore intravista
è materia immigrante, flusso *peligroso*
frutto ibridato - era mela divina -
a marcire negli angoli

sorvolo l'area desertica, le oasi antropiche
                                        della distanza
anche l'area temperata, antropofaga
                              a macchie urbane

A FOREST BREEZE BLOWS ON MY CHEEKS

a forest breeze blows on my cheeks
I'm flying
exploring a dream arms splayed
we are voices flocking
as if en route on a path of air
with our shell our pilgrim's robe
        evening radiating on the pulse of song

I'm writing
about my room, its uncertainty
in the soft glow of the screen
that steals the voice, *emoticons*
replacing word-caresses on my skin   skin
if only it would shed
pride competition
the now plasmatic fraction of evil
oh how many of us are deprived
and the dose of love we glimpse
is immigrant stuff, a perilous flux
hybrid fruit - apple that once was divine -
rotting in a corner

I hover over desert ground, the anthropic oasis
                                        of distance
over temperate anthropophagous ground too
                                        dappled with towns

sto scrivendo
della mia illusione sulle fondamenta
molle cemento in lenta subsidenza del desiderio
sentirmi lambire da lingue-incendio   lingue
a parlarsi, poi
                    solo scintille   buio

il risveglio sarà per-voce, ancora   voce
canto battesimale, onda di madre
scalderà d'accoglienza sangue, cellule   cellule
cresceranno ancora nel timore di spegnersi
nella tragedia che ancora accade
l'odio l'incendio il trasporto dei padri sulle spalle
Enea in cammino fino all'Antartide

sto guardando
la foresta giù che lampeggia
il verde corpo disteso beneaugurante
a vegliare sui flussi naturali, sui nuovi nati
- potrebbero tecnomorire - o puri
tornare a correre sulla pianura   salvarsi
di diluvio in diluvio

I'm writing
about the foundations having deceived me
soft cement subsiding slowly with my desire
to feel fire-tongues licking me   tongues
speaking to each other, then
                    mere sparks   darkness

we'll be woken by the voice, once more   voice
baptismal song, a maternal wave
will warmly welcome blood, cells   cells
will grow again afraid of being extinguished
in the tragedy that is still unfolding
hatred fire fathers carried on our backs
Aeneas en route to Antarctica

I'm looking
at the forest flickering below
its green body auspiciously outstretched
watching over the natural flow, over the newborn
- they could die a technodeath - or remain pure
running through the plain once more   be saved
between one deluge and the next

LO CHIAMANO ABITARE

lo chiamano abitare: si rotola
sul confine tra deserto e una terra
insolente di promesse, sterile
per dismisura di pianto
eufrate e tigri insabbiati
nel salino di lacrime
perdo lo sguardo smémoro la luce
- sclera bianca -
non riconosco la tua casa che brucia
la tua voce che calma

è l'amen della notte questo cielo
polvere raggelata
accade con l'imperfezione annunciata
il riproporsi ostinato del sangue
il dibattersi vano di parole nell'inchiostro dei secoli
storia illudedelude
verità tradiscetrasgredisce:
due civette dai grandi occhi impassibili
stanno -sfrontate- sui Grandi Libri
su ogni colonna miliare o torre ambigua
di avvistamento di controllo
minaretocupolacampanile

THEY CALL IT LIVING

they call it living: we spin
on the border between desert and an insolent
land of promises, made sterile
by an excess of sorrow
euphrates and tigris buried in sand
in the salt of tears
I lose my sight the memory of light
- white sclera -
unable to recognize your house burning
your calming voice

this sky, frozen dust
is the night's amen
the obstinate reemergence of blood
the vain flapping of words on the ink of centuries
come with announced imperfection
history disappointsdeceives
truth betraystransgresses: two owls
with their large impassive eyes
pose - impudent - on the Great Books
on every milepost, or ambiguous
lookout or watch tower
minaretcupolacampanille

tu solo mi raccogli, amore
nel tuo cesto di scintille
in tempuscoli di tuono

siamo mandorle di luce nella coppa del buio
minime caparbie vibrazioni
lasceremo tracce di un approdo
un viluppo tremante al riparo

you alone pick me up, sweetheart
in your basket of sparks
in the briefest moments of thunder

we are almonds of light in the cup of darkness
little stubborn vibrations
we'll leave traces of our mooring
a trembling embrace in a shelter

PAESEMONDO

Un paese che si chiama Cocumola è
come avere le mani sporche di farina
e un portoncino verde color limone.
Uomini con camicie silenziose
fanno un nodo al fazzoletto
per ricordarsi del cuore
Vittorio Bodini

ritorno pellegrina
a uno spazio d'equilibrio
sommerso di luce orientale
mia casa-paese protetta che protegge
senza recinti

attraversarla è penetrare
una calda coerenza
un racconto vivo che non si ferma
oltrepassa i muri

partire è lasciarsi dietro un mondo
le sentinelle accese su ogni soglia
non atterrisce nessuna terra dei giganti
flebile ogni canto di sirene

la nostra piazza è centro che dilata
cerchi di parole, urti semplici
a dipanare vita, tenere accesi i fuochi

VILLAGEWORLD

A village called Cocumola is
like having your hands covered in flour
and a green lemon-colored wicket door.
Men wearing silent shirts
tie a knot in their handkerchief
so as to remember the heart
Vittorio Bodini

I return as a pilgrim
to a place of equilibrium
submerged in eastern light
my protected home-village protecting
without fences

crossing it means penetrating
cosy coherence
a living story that never ends
that transcends walls

going away means leaving a world behind
with watchmen alert at every doorstep
no land of giants instills fear
every siren's song is faint

our piazza is a hub that expands
circles of words, simple knocks
that unravel life, keep the fires burning

quelle foto in cortile, da bambini
occhi neri vivissimi
frenesia di giochi mai interrotti
ai quattro cantoni del mondo

tatuata casa-paese che con noi cammina
ovunque, sotto l'unico cielo scritto dalle stelle
paesemondo
per vivere, con-vivere

those photos in the courtyard, us as kids
        with our vivid black eyes
the frenzy of games never interrupted
tig in the four corners of the earth

tattooed home-village that walks with us
everywhere, under the one sky inscribed with stars
                    villageworld
                  to live in, love in

SARAI FAMOSA

accende la stanza intera, dal video
frenetica
la tua pelle in moto, giovane e inerme
aggredisce
invaso da suoni lucidi il corpo
inconsapevole trasmuta
sintetico

come hanno potuto dileguarsi
tutte le fiabe che ti avevano nutrita
arretrare tutte le leggende
addensarti Nausicaa iperflessuosa
nel moto convulso che ti svela
occhismarrita efémera di una notte
fragile di troppa attesa

poi ti sembra di udirlo, dal buio
oltre l'ultima fila, il fruscio
qualcosa-qualcuno
                        che s'allontana

Raccolgo da terra braccia, gambe
ti riassemblo a fatica
                        per un altro palco

YOU'LL BE A STAR

the whole room lights up, on the video
frenetic
your skin in motion, young and defenseless
attacks
invaded by gleaming sounds your body
unconsciously transmutes
synthetically

how could all the fairytales
that fed you have dispersed
all the legends withdrawn
made you, super-supple Nausicaä, heavy
in the convulsive moves that reveal you
as ephemeral, losteyed for one night
frail from so much waiting

then you think you hear it, in the dark
beyond the last row, a rustle
someone-something
                                        leaving

I pick up fallen arms, legs
painstakingly rebuild you
                                        for some other stage

AVESSI AVUTO FIGLIE

le avrei chiamate con nomi di fiori
Amarilli Artemisia Ninfea risvegliate dal mito
Salvia Veronica Eufrasia benedictae

nel giardino dei giorni, un fiore quotidiano
con cui ridere del mondo e cantare riordinando la casa
- ragnatele smagliate dall'urto dolce del canto -
mi sarebbe bastato, anche se
i fiori mai rivelano il loro breve segreto
solo a sera raccontano
aromistupori del giorno
e il più giovane in boccio può interrogarti
sul senso ambiguo del fuoco
e tu non puoi che rispondere
serve alla civiltà

HAD I HAD DAUGHTERS

I would have named them after flowers
Amaryllis Artemisia Lily waking them from myth
benedictae Sage Veronica Euphrasy

in the garden of days, a daily flower
to laugh with about the world and sing through the chores
- cobwebs ripped by the sweet impact of song -
would have made me happy, even if
flowers never reveal their fleeting secret
recount the heady scents of the day
only at night
and the youngest, still budding, might quiz you
on the ambiguous nature of fire
and all you can say is
it's useful for civilisation

petali fuori posto avrei sistemato
aerei ikebana avrei insegnato
ceduto a nuove geometrie-autonomie
sofferto pure dello sconfinare
di profumi ribelli
fior di progetti avremmo ideato
perché i fiori sanno di simmetrie e fantasticano
di volatile rugiada e foreste imbattibili
le nostre asimmetrie e dismisure
trasferite sui rami, ingoiate dai venti
i fiori accettano
la brevità del colore, lo spegnersi
del fruscio vitale al tramonto

lasciarmi sfiorire
appoggiata a uno stelo filiale
attendere
sull'orlo dei calici la fioritura

I would have tidied wayward petals
taught them airy ikebanas
given in to new geometries, autonomies
even endured rebellious perfumes
wafting across the boundaries
our best plans would have flowered
because flowers know about symmetry and fantasize
about the volatile dew and invincible forests
our asymmetries and excesses
transferred to the branches, swallowed by the winds
flowers accept
the brevity of colour, the dimming
of life's rustle as the sun sets

I'm withering now
against a filial stalk
waiting on the edge of the calyx
for the bloom

NOI ETRUSCHE

da voi parole- pietra, telepatiche
perché lungo il tempo
mai abbiamo smesso di parlarci fitto
sul bordo di labbra in sorriso
coprendovi lo sposo - lui convinto -
col braccio le spalle per il viaggio

noi furtive e ironiche
abbiamo già solcato quel mare languido
nella decisione che sarà più largo e pacifico
e maternale tutto ciò che da aruspici
abbiamo divinato
l'attesa a noi si addice
e la festa, nel tempo di Horta delle messi
e di Feronia che fa correre in seno il latte
ancora per le mensa d'aprile prepariamo
l'agnello primo nato
e mandorle e miele

la danza a noi si addice, muove
solo per corde e voci, a ottundere
l'ultima eco di lame - fluttuano
ancora, agli uomini dietro la fronte -
a cancellargli il canone del rosso
rossa pelle di rosse vittorie
cantiamo il ruotare di lune
sulle ombre azzurre dei rami dei nidi

WE ETRUSCAN WOMEN

from you we have stone-words, telepathic
given that over time we've
never stopped talking to each other intently
from the corners of smiling lips
with your husband's arm - confidently -
round your shoulders for the journey

we, furtive and ironic
have already sailed that sentimental sea
knowing that everything we've foreseen
as aruspices will be wider, more pacific
and maternal
the wait suits us
and the feast, in Horta's season of harvests
and Feronia's that makes milk flow in our breast
once more for the April table we prepare
the first born lamb
                                        and almonds and honey

the dance suits us, it moves
only with chords and voices, blunting
the last echo of blades - still
floating in men's heads -
erasing the red tradition
the red skin of red victories
we sing the moon's rotation
on the blue shadows of branches, of nests

noi etrusche oggi, fianco a fianco
a liquefare il ferro delle spade
in conche d'esorcismo
e parole e parole a modellare
la vita in forme vive:
sostegni per la vigna, sedie
                    per i racconti della sera

we etruscan women today, side by side
liquefying all the iron of swords
in exorcistic bowls
and word upon word we model
life into living forms:
stakes for the vineyard, chairs
                for night-time stories

UN INFINITESIMO BIANCO

(Dal tg RAI del 26 dicembre 2008:
Prende fuoco una baracca nella pineta di Castelfusano.
Nell'incendio muoiono una donna romena di
33 anni col suo bambino.)

un infinitesimo bianco
un assestamento del pensiero - brevissimo -
sulla rovente prossimità del volo
sull'ultima tessera a comporsi

- ha tre anni mio figlio
e un respiro di resina nel sonno
ecco che allatta alla mia cenere
sul palmo delle mani abbiamo un marchio
a fuoco, di pinoli e bacche d'agrifoglio
ieri ne raccoglievamo ridendo
in lite con i merli -

A SPLIT SECOND OF LIGHT

(From RAI News, 26 December 2008:
A fire has broken out in a hut in the Castelfusano pine forest.
A 33 year old Romanian woman and her child
have died in the blaze.)

a split second of light
a thought settles - ever so briefly -
over the burning proximity of flight
over the last piece of the mosaic to be laid

- he's three years old, my son
and breathes resin in his sleep
now he's suckling on my ashes
on the palms of our hands we have the flaming
mark of pine nuts and holly berries
yesterday we were laughing as we collected them,
fighting off the blackbirds -

UN LABIRINTO INCISO IN LINEARE B

un labirinto inciso in lineare B
sigillo interno
da sempre nasce con noi
ci segue ci segna

come nel gioco a quadri quando
disegnavamo in terra una campana
vita percorsa a balzi, intrico che dipana
bambine-Ariadni attente
a non calpestare il limite
mentre ostinati i piedi battevano
sulle sbarre del mondo
i voli, gli arresti smarriti

un labirinto in sinuosa traccia danzante
che di continuo inverte il moto
in ricordo dello sperdimento scuro
della biforme vinta creatura
ancora oggi mito
ogm-chimera

A LABYRINTH ETCHED IN LINEAR B

a labyrinth etched in linear B
an internal seal
from the beginning born with us
following us branding us

like the hopscotch squares
we drew on the ground, a life-path
travelled in hops, the intricacy unravelling
we, little Ariadnes careful
not to cross the boundary
while our feet obstinately beat
against the bars of the world
the flights, the bewildered stops

a labyrinth in its sinuous dancing trail
that keeps inverting motion
recalling the dark disorientation
of the defeated bi-form creature
the GMO-chimera
still a myth today

ci salva la donna dei gomitoli
signora del labirinto
con le sette stanze dello stupore
nella sua cavità delle nascite
offrirle un vaso ebbro di miele
un grazie danzato tutti legati a un filo
nel buio dei meandri chiaro s'avvolge
si svolge irresistibile
uno scialle si agita nella danza del ragno
Aracne annoda e snoda la sua tela d'incontri

we are saved by the lady with the ball of fleece
mistress of the labyrinth
with the seven rooms of wonder
in her cavity of births
we'd like to offer her a drunken cup of honey
a dance of gratitude all linked by a thread
in the darkness of the meanders a shawl winds
irresistably unwinds
flaps in the spider's dance
Arachne knots and unknots her web of encounters

TECHNE
(come si scolpisce un santo)

centrali le mani nel cercare
la chiave d'una porta materica
mentre indietreggia l'aria e accade
il pigreco dell'attesa
sbozzato profilo di padremadre
pietra di accumulato amore eviscerata
forma improvvisa che respira
                                        altro occhio

energia palpabile di roccia, vibrata
da nodi antichissimi, disfatti
febbrili polso e dita
segnano l'aria di voli di brusii
soffiano dall'incavo nebbiolina marmorea
come mano di madre che deterge
del latte il mento del neonato

centrale, il santo Kevin
sasso addensato in beatitudine
nella fissità illimite obbediente
parolapietra di venerazione
a braccia tese il santo Kevin
col palmo aperto fuori dalla finestra
a far da nido al merlo che vi si era posato
                                        fino alla schiusa

TECHNIQUE
(how to sculpt a saint)

central to finding the key
to a door made of matter are hands
while air recedes
and the awaited greek pi appears
the rough profile of a motherfather
accumulated love in stone, eviscerated
an unexpected form that breathes
another eye

rock's palpable energy, throbbing
from ancient nodes, undone
feverish pulse and fingers
etch the air with flights and murmurs
blow marbled mist from the hollow
like a mother's hand wiping milk
from the newborn's chin

central is Saint Kevin
stone made solid in its bliss
in its limitless obedient fixity
stone-speech to be venerated
with arms outstretched Saint Kevin
opens his palm outside the window
as a nest for the blackbird that alighted there
till it was time to hatch

NONOSTANTE IL SOLITO PAESAGGIO

nonostante il solito paesaggio
il nuovo deve compiersi
assumerò il tuo viso a mio nirvana
dall'angolo acutissimo della consistenza
i tuoi occhi
                frecce di parole
mi raggiungevano
fino a ferirmi di rinascita

rimane ora il silenzio
tuo aereo ensemble di suoni
l'evanescenza cauta della bellezza
questo moto supernaturale del corpo
consonante alla salita di questa linfa d'aprile
alla ferocia struggente dell'abbandono
dicevi mai sarà tempo di lacerazioni
solo tepore d'onde in cui tuffarsi
seguendo l'espandersi dei cerchi

- ancora la tua voce -
ora che giocallegro a calcetto
mio ragazzo nuovo delle tue cornee
i tuoi occhi
                fatti per sommuovere

DESPITE THE USUAL LANDSCAPE

despite the usual landscape
I must find new ways of moving on
I'll feign your face in my nirvana
from the most vivid angle of your being
your eyes
            word arrows
used to reach me
till they wounded me with rebirth

now there is silence
your airy ensemble of sounds
the evanescense of beauty
this supernatural movement of the body
in harmony with the rise of this April lymph
with the disconsolate ferocity of abandonment
you used to say there'll be no more time for grief
only the warmth of waves to dive into
following the rings as they spread

- still your voice -
now that this boy happy-kicks
his ball, renewed with your corneas
your eyes
            made to move

NASCITA

per Annina, figlia di Maria Grazia.

il tuo tuffo albale l'odore
di nebbia del premondo
ti hanno lavato via dalla pelle
la vernice del caos
sei nel mare d'ossigeno e d'occhi
coi pugni stretti bussavi
che si lacerasse il morbido scafo
il cielo si è incurvato
sul tuo battere di vele al passaggio

facile seguire la corrente
su scie di madre-musica, voce ag-Graziata
sei scivolata in un fascio di papaveri
su questa terramara di palafitte
che ancora ondeggia, non sorregge i giacigli

ti siano dolci il canto-latte, i fiori sulla riva
le curve morbidissime dei ponti
ti sia chiara la luce che già bevi
nella percezione di minime
costellazioni - scintillano
i denti di Arturo che sorride -
e già vuoi sulla pelle a tatuarti
le prime gocce ardenti di parole

felici ore a te, planata
sulle nostre ginocchia in preghiera
volerti prendere per mano
e tu a guidare

BIRTH

for Maria Grazia's daughter, Annina

your dive at dawn   the scent
of mist from the pre-world
they've washed the waxy chaos
from your skin
you're in a sea of oxygen and eyes
with clenched fists you knocked
so the soft hull would tear
the sky curved round your beating sails
as they went by

it's easy to flow with the tide
in the wake of mother-music, its Grace-ful voice
you slipped into a host of poppies
in our terramara built on stilts
still bobbing, unable to hold up our pallets

may the milk-song, flowers on the riverbank
the gentle curves of bridges be sweet for you
may the light you already drink
be clear as you perceive the tiniest
of constellations - Arturo's teeth
sparkling as he smiles at you -
and on your skin you already want to tattoo
the first ardent shower of words

may your hours be joyful, planing
on our knees bent in prayer
wanting to take your hand
so you can lead

SEMPRE PIU SPESSO DIMENTICO

sempre più spesso dimentico
dove ho parcheggiato la macchina
si somigliano tutte le strade
nel sentore del mare che avanza
nel confondente richiamo delle pietre
dall'ultima riva   un brusio
familiare soffia sulla nuca
sulle vele inarcate a proteggere
la mia traversata

là respira, in attesa
questa mia terra del moto selvatico
si stacca dal continente, in silenzio
come la zattera di Saramago

là devo accompagnare
tutti coloro che mi sono partiti
salvare le voci le mappe
i consigli di viaggio i contagi di luce

ecco perché con pazienza
da qualche parte la mia macchina aspetta

INCREASINGLY I FORGET

increasingly I forget
where I've parked the car
the streets all look the same
with their sense of the sea encroaching
with the confusing call of stones
from the last riverbed   a familiar
buzzing blows on the nape of my neck
on full sails that protect
my crossing

that's where this land of mine breathes
with its wild motion, waiting,
it detaches from the continent, in silence
like Saramago's raft

that's where I must accompany
everyone who is gone from me
save the voices the maps
the travel advice the contagions of light

this is why somewhere out there
my car is patiently waiting

AL CAPOLINEA

salire sul 160, capolinea paziente
tra i due platani - sempre alla stessa ora -
muta solo l'umore, come le nuvole
                        uguale la mancanza

Il posto che preferisco è quello in fondo
al centro della fila orizzontale, il migliore
per assistere al film, puntuale:
piccola folla composta, in parte seduta in parte in piedi
si parla con sguardi, diffida di chi le sta accanto
        lo ama   lo cerca   lo urta
nell'inclinazione sottile dei corpi
ciecamente consegnata alla fatalità del moto
ognuno coprendo il suo cosmico tratto di asfaltocielo

E non so perché mi commuove
tutto di questo bus fendinuvole:
la marcia il freno i sobbalzi il contrasto dell'aria
il riflesso sul vetro del pianto stellare
il turbinio del sangue sottopelle
- nostalgia del bigbang - se il cuore
sta meditando di rallentare, predisporsi al viaggio

AT THE FIRST STOP

getting on the 160, the patient first stop
between two plane-trees - always at the same time -
only the mood changes, like the clouds
                                        while loss remains

my favourite seat is that one down the back
in the middle of the horizontal row, the best
for watching the film that punctually unfolds:
a small prim crowd, some sitting some standing
chatting with glances, mistrusting whoever's beside them
            loving   searching   knocking against them
in the gentle give of bodies
blindly resigned to the inevitability of motion
everyone covering his own cosmic bit of asphaltsky

and I don't know why everything
about this cloud-cutting bus moves me:
the speed the breaks the jolts the contrasting air
the reflection of wailing stars on the glass
the swirling of blood under the skin
- a hankering for the big bang - while my heart
is thinking of slowing down, preparing for the journey

Guardo il treno correre nelle pupille di chi mi è davanti:
piccole locomotive accendersi - un bimbo mi fissa curioso -
curiosa anch'io di vedere la sua fermata di scintille
decido di non scendere ancora
mi abbarbico al sostegno di uscita
(il viale continua oltre la piazza ?)

Infine che cosa ho fatto se non
lasciarmi andare sulla scia dei nomi?
amicheamici che mi aiutate a scenderesalire
gioisco del vostro tocco   non so darvi in cambio
che qualche ritmo e un brusìo
di un arrivo lontano
                    che già è partenza

I watch the train go by in the pupils of the person facing me:
little engines lighting up - a curious child stares at me -
as I am curious to see his sparkling stop
I decide not to get off yet
cling to the pole at the exit
(does the route go beyond the piazza?)

in the end what have I done except
wander willingly over a wake of names?
menwomen friends who help me get on and off
I rejoice in your touch   in return can only give
the odd rhythm and the hum
of my arrival long ago
                                        that is already a departure

UNA LINGUASILENZIO FELICE LARGA PIOVE

una linguasilenzio felice larga piove
penetra cantapetali dentro   nel
dentro innocente sanguelinfahumus
permea senso   senza
metallo che risuoni

da muro a muro da spina a spina
i dispersi al tocco sussultano si stringono
di fronte è la gelida notte
lontane le due torri come mammuth
emersi domani dalle nevi

ecco che galleggia sopra di me un Atlante
di sperdimento   avvampa
così intensa la musica
ha forma d'arpa il telaio
tutti quei pesi di terracotta
a piombo come ghigliottine
ora stanno in levità di vibrafoni
nel primitivo piegarsi delle spighe
spose che vanno, culle
luce sul confine tra carezza e lama

A LANGUAGESILENCE LONG AND HAPPY RAINS

a languagesilence long and happy rains
penetrates petalsongs inside   in the
innocent inside, bloodlymphhumus
permeates meaning with   without
metal that might resound

from wall to wall from thorn to thorn
dispersed people are startled by touch, reunite
faced with the freezing night
the two towers are gone like mammoths
emerging tomorrow from the snow

now the Atlas mountains float
over me   bewildering, burning
the music so intense
the loom looks like a harp
all those terracotta weights
like leaden guillotines
now light as vibraphones
among the primitive bending of wheat
brides ambling, cradles
light on the border between caresses and blades

abbiamo consegnato le ferite
insieme alle armi, preferito la festa
le lunghissime tavole sonore
il miele delle nozze diffuso
tornare nudi su terra nuda
farsi gola d'agnello mille volte
se occorre ancora sangue
per il gocciolio della fine

porte del mondo che ritornano alberi
città come campi da seminare
illuminati a regno   piove
un silenzio-beatitudo
sonno infantile, lava che pietrifica

una fila di pietre da riscrivere

we've handed over the wounds
and our arms, we've chosen the feast
its long boisterous tables
wedding honey flowing
we'll return naked to naked earth
be the lamb's throat a thousand times over
should blood be required once more
to drip slowly to an end

doors of the world back to trees
cities as fields to be sown
lit like kingdoms   it's raining
beatitude-silence
a child's sleep, lava that petrifies

there's still a row of rocks to be rewritten

ABOUT THE AUTHOR

ANNAMARIA FERRAMOSCA was born in Tricase (Lecce), but currently lives in Rome where she works as a nutritional biologist. She is the author of five poetry collections: *Il versante vero,* Fermenti, Rome, 1999; *Porte di terra dormo,* Dialogo Libri, Como, 2001; *Porte/Doors,* Edizioni del Leone, Venice, 2002, with English translations by Anamaría Crowe Serrano and Riccardo Duranti; *Curve di livello,* Marsilio, Venice, 2006; *Paso doble,* Empiria, Rome, 2006, a bilingual collection of "dual" poems co-written with Anamaría Crowe Serrano and translated into English by Riccardo Duranti.

As a writer of critical essays and reviews, her texts have appeared in several print and online journals, including *Poesia, La Mosca di Milano, La Clessidra, Hebenon, Le voci della Luna, Poiesis, La colpa di scrivere, Leggendaria, Noi donne, FreeVerse,* poiein.it, and vicoacitillo.net, where reviews of her own work have also appeared.

Some of her poems have been anthologised in *L'altro Novecento,* 1999, ed. Vittoriano Esposito; *Appunti critici,* 2002, ed. Giorgio Linguaglossa; *Tradizione e ricerca nella poesia contemporanea*, 2008, ed. Sandro Montalto.

She has adjudicated at the Davide Maria Turoldo Poetry Prize, and currently collaborates with the Clepsydra Edizioni e-book which aims to provide online exposure for new poets.

CRITICAL REVIEWS

Antomarini, B., Cocciolillo, B., Filardi, R., Grego, A. (eds.) *InVerse Italian Poets in Translation,* John Cabot University Press, Rome, 2007

Barbano, M., "Il versante vero di una poetessa salentina", in *La Gazzetta del Mezzogiorno,* August 2, 1999

Battilana, M., "Esercizi Letterari", in *La Nuova Tribuna Letteraria,* #48, 1997

Benassi, L., "*Curve di livello",* in *Noi Donne,* #3, 2007

Bertoni, R., "Annamaria Ferramosca's Doors into words and silence", in *Translation Ireland,* vol. 15, p. 2, 2002

Bisutti, D., "Paso Doble" in *Poesia,* Crocetti, # 221, November 2007

Calandrone, M.G., "*Curve di livello*", in *La Mosca di Milano*, #15, 2006
Cannillo, L., "*Curve di livello*", in *Le voci della luna*, #37, 2007
Cara, D., "La parola convocata", in *Laboratorio delle Arti*, pp.386-87, Milan, 1998
Cara, D., "Annamaria Ferramosca- *Il versante vero*", in *Punto di vista*, p.23, Jan-March 2000
Carlino, M., in www.literary.it , #12, 2007
Cenciarelli, G., "Irlanda-Italia: esperimenti in versi", in www.sinestetica.net, December 2006
Cenciarelli, G., "Irlanda e Italia: un Paso Doble in versi", in www.vibriss bollettino.net , October 2006
Crowe Serrano, A., "Place in Contemporary Italian Poetry: Anna Maria Robustelli, Annamaria Ferramosca, Patrizia Cavalli, Sara Ventroni, Silvia Bre", in *Free Verse*, Spring 2008
Demarchi, S., "*Il versante vero*", in *La Nuova Tribuna Letteraria*, # 55, 1999
Di Stasi, D., "La distruzione del nulla", in *Fermenti*, #221, pp.113-14, 1999
Esposito, V., "Annamaria Ferramosca" in *L'altro novecento – La poesia Centro-Meridionale e insulare*, Bastoni, Foggia, pp.618-20, 1999
Folliero, S., "Il versante vero di Annamaria Ferramosca", in *Fermenti*, #222, 2000
Folliero, S., "Annamaria Ferramosca, Curve di livello" in *Hebenon*, #7-8, Nov 06-May 07
Franceschini, L., Renzi, R., Tuzet, G., "Se la poesia attraversa la natura" in *Argo*, #13, 2007
Gattoni, L., "Curve di livello" in *Poetry wave*, www.vicoacitillo.net, 2007
Gros-Pietro, S., "Annamaria Ferramosca - *Porte/Doors*", in *Vernice*, #23, Genesi Editrice, Turin, 2002
Guastella, A., "Note sulla poesia contemporanea - Annamaria Ferramosca", in *Cultura & Libri*, #132, 2001
Lanza, L., "La parola fuggevole di Annamaria Ferramosca", in *La Clessidra*, #1, 2007
Lanza, L., "Annamaria Ferramosca - Curve di livello" in *L'Immaginazione*, #233, September 2007
La Rocca, A., "Il versante vero di Annamaria Ferramosca" in *Hyria*, #83-84, 1999
Lenisa, M.g., "*Curvedi livello*", in *Punto d'Incontro*, #3-4, Sept-Dec 2006
Levante, D., "Una poetica odissea della quotidianità" in *La Gazzetta del Mezzogiorno*, September 19, 2006
Liguori, E., "Poesia-Pane", in *Il Paese nuovo*, April 1, 2009

Linguaglossa, G., "Annamaria Ferramosca" in *Poiesis*, #21-22, pp. 35-38, 2001
Linguaglossa, G., "Ferramosca, Annamaria", in *Appunti Critici: La poesia italiana del tardo Novecento tra conformismi e nuove proposte*, Edizioni Scettro del Re, pp.299-300, Rome, 2002
Lo Passo, A., "*Curve di livello*", in *La colpa di scrivere*, p. 8, Oct-Dec 2006
Maffia, D., "I poeti del terzo millennio", in *Punto d'incontro*, #3, Sept-Dec 2000
Maffia, D., "Annamaria Ferramosca" in *Poiesis*, #21-22, pp.35-38, 2001
Maffia, D., "Porte/Doors – Annamaria Ferramosca" in *Poiesis*, #26-27, 2003
Maffia, D., "Ferramosca, Annamaria", in *Poeti Italiani verso il nuovo millennio*, p.307, Scettro del Re, Roma 2002
Mestas, J.P., "A livre ouvert" in *Jalons*, #74, 2003
Mestas, J.P., "Italie: Annamaria Ferramosca" #75, 2003
Mestas, J.P., "Italie: Annamaria Ferramosca" #78, 2004
Miano, G., "Ferramosca Annamaria", in *Contributi per la Storia della Letteratura italiana-Il secondo Novecento*, Guido Miano Editore, vol.III, pp.276-77, Milan, 2004
Montalto, S., "Annamaria Ferramosca" in *Tradizione e Ricerca nella poesia contemporanea*, pp.196-7, Edizioni Joker, Novi Ligure, 2008
Mugnaini, I., "Punto analisi esegetiche", in *Punto d'incontro*, #5-6, Sept-Dec 2002
Mugnaini, I., "Annamaria Ferramosca – Porte/Doors" in *La Clessidra*, #2, 2003
Musetti, G., "*Curvedi livello*", in *Leggere Donna*, #125, Nov-Dec 2006
Nesti, W., *"Porte/Doors"*, in *Punto di Vista*, #35, 2003
Piazza, R., "*Porte/Doors*" in *Gradiva*, #25, 2004
Poli, G., "*Porte/Doors*", in *Punto di Vista*, #37, 2003
Rebecchi, E., *Quando il poeta è donna*, pp.33-44, Blu di Prussia, Piacenza 2002
Rienzi, A., "*Curve di livello*", in *Scorpione letterario*, #6-7, 2007
Rizzo, M., "Annamaria Ferramosca-*Il Versante vero*", in *Sìlarus*, #214, March-April 2001
Rizzo, M., "*Curve di livello*" in *Il Segnale*, #77, 2007
Robustelli, A.M., "Curve di livello" in *La Mosca di Milano*, #16, May 2007
Salibra, E., "*Porte/Doors*" in *Soglie*, #3, December 2002
Sarrocco, G., "*Il versante vero*", in *Il Tempo*, May 23, 1999
Simonelli, F., "*Il versante vero*" in *Poesia*, #132, Crocetti, October 1999
Simonelli, F., "*Porte/Doors*" in Poesia, #104, September 2002

Starace Pietroni, E., "Ventagli di palme su un asfalto di fuoco", in *La Gazzetta di Parma*, January 3, 2007
Stifani, A., "Annamaria Ferramosca - *Il versante vero*", in *Punto d'incontro*, #2, May-August 2000
Wilson, J., "*Paso Doble*" in *New Hope International Review*, www.geraldengland.co.uk, 2007
Zaccaria, O., *Porte/Doors"*, in *La Nuova Tribuna Letteraria*, #71, 2003

ACKNOWLEDGMENTS

Chelsea Editions thanks the editors of the following journals, in which some of these poems appeared: *Italian Poetry Review*, *Free Verse*, *La Clessidra*, *Le voci della luna*, *Il Fiacre*, *poiein.it*

ABOUT THE TRANSLATOR

ANAMARÍA CROWE SERRANO is Irish and lives in Dublin. She has worked with several languages for many years – translating, writing, reading, teaching. Among the poets she has translated are Seamus Heaney, Brendan Kennelly, Gerardo Beltrán, Elsa Cross, Valerio Magrelli, Patrizia Cavalli. Her first collection of short stories, *Dall'altra parte*, was published by Leconte in 2003, followed in the same year by a one-act play, *L'interprete*, (Delta3 Edizioni). She has also published with Annamaria Ferramosca an experimental poetic dialogue in Italian and English titled *Paso Doble* (Empirìa, 2006). In 2008, the British publisher Shearsman released her first collection of poetry, *Femispheres*. The recipient of two awards from the Arts Council of Ireland for her writing, she also took joint third prize with Riccardo Duranti in 2002 at the John Dryden Translation Competition (sponsored by the British Comparative Literature Association and the British Centre for Literary Translation) for their translation of Valerio Magrelli's *Instructions on How to Read a Newspaper*, subsequently published by Chelsea Editions, 2008, under the longer title *Instructions on How to Read a Newspaper and Other Poems*, with further translations by Anthony Molino.

Rinaldo Caddeo | **Siren's Song** | Selected Poetry and Prose 1989-2009

ChelseaEditions

RINALDO CADDEO
Siren's Song: Selected Poetry and Prose, 1989—2009
Translated by Adria Bernardi
Illustrations by Salvatore Carbone
Paperback, 283 pages, $20 ISBN 978-0-9823849-1-6

RINALDO CADDEO, born in Milan in 1952 where he resides and teaches in a technical institute, has published four collections of poetry *(Le fionde del gioco e del vuoto, Narciso, Calendario di sabbia, Dialogo con l'ombra)*, one collection of short-short stories *(La lingua del camaleonte)*, and one of aphorisms *(Etimologia del caos)*. Piccola Biblioeca di Odissea has published his short story *Apocalisse 2009.*

Siren's Song: Selected Poetry and Prose 1989-2009 is from *La lingua del camaleonte* (Manni Editore, 2002), *Narciso* (Forum/ Quinta Generazione, 1989), *Calendario di sabbia* (NCE, 1997), and *I mostri* (new unpublished poetry). His prizes for poetry are "Romagna" for *Narciso,* 1989, and in 1998 "Delta Poesia" for *Calendario di sabbia.* He is author of critical essays, book reviews, short stories, aphorisms, translations and poetry published in numerous literary magazines. He is an associate editor of the biannual *La mosca di Milano.*

"A beautiful investigation of the alternative to life and death, into the truth of tragicality, of understanding hard won, and of thought illuminated. A poem for brain shocks, visions and encounters with elemental emblems of time and being: the moth, the bat, the infant, the statue, the tree, the hare, the leaf, the wind. One reads "Siren's Song," "Foreigners," "The Wild Beast," and many other poems, with particular joy." —*Giorgio Barberi-Squarotti*

available through **ChelseaEditionsBooks.org** *or* **Amazon.com**

the dragonfly
A Selection of Poems: 1953-1981
AMELIA ROSSELLI

ChelseaEditions

AMELIA ROSSELLI
The Dragonfly: A Selection of Poems: 1953—1981
Translated by Giuseppe Leporace and Deborah Woodard
Paperback, 275 pages, $20   ISBN 978-0-9823849-0-9

AMELIA ROSSELLI was born in Paris in 1930 to anti-Fascist parents who had fled Italy. Her father was assassinated in Normandy by Mussolini's henchmen when Rosselli was seven years old. "The daughter with the devastated heart" grew up in Europe and the United States, eventually settling in Rome. In fierce and incandescent verse that draws upon the languages she learned in exile, Rosselli explores the intersection of the traumatized self with the psyche of the post-WWII generation. Rosselli committed suicide in Rome on February 11, 1996. Garzanti published her *Collected Poems* in 1997.

"Anti-fascist, Jewish, multi-lingual, a perennial exile, Amelia Rosselli is one of the great poets of the 20th century. Her tragic yet consolatory voice is comparable to Celan, Bachmann, Char, Pasternak, Akmatova, and Plath, all of whom she loved. Her work with language is always the result of a painstaking attempt to give to the reader an accurate sense of a painful, oppressive and violent reality experienced or witnessed directly, a reality that Rosselli wishes to expose, resist and call into question. Fascism, World War II, the Holocaust, the Cold War, right-wing political brutality, social injustice, the oppressiveness of media and consumer culture, the obtuse selfishness of the bourgeoisie, are all realities that her texts evoke. To read her is to embark on an unforgettable journey of suffering and redemption."—*Lucia Re*

available through **ChelseaEditionsBooks.org** *or* **Amazon.com**

VALERIO MAGRELLI

Edited by Anthony Molino
Translated from the Italian by
Riccardo Duranti
Anamaría Crowe Serrano
Anthony Molino
Introduction by Peter Hainsworth

Instructions on How to Read a Newspaper and Other Poems

ChelseaEditions

VALERIO MAGRELLI
Instructions on How to Read a Newspaper and Other Poems
Edited by Anthony Molino
Translated from the Italian by Riccardo Duranti,
Anamaría Crowe Serrano, and Anthony Molino
With an introduction by Peter Hainsworth and an
afterword by Riccardo Duranti.
Paperback, 366 pages, $20 ISBN 0-9725271-7-6

"Magrelli's *Instructions on How to Read a Newspaper* is a striking, ambitious, and indeed ingenious creation, evidence of a poetic strategy that daringly spearheads and remains at the forefront of Italian poetry today."—*Prof. Peter Hainsworth, Oxford University (from his Introduction)*

"His poetry is a soliloquy written with a pencil and small notebook, during the latest and most silent hours of the night. It's a poetry that looks at itself, but at the sight of its thought, vanishes."—*Octavio Paz*

"I used to read a great many Italian poets. Nowhere near as many in recent years—though I've seen things by a young poet that I like very much. His name is Magrelli."—*Joseph Brodsky*

"In the good-natured ease with which he shows off his mastery of the traditional tools of his trade, here is a writer whose energy and gifts open a doorway onto an expansive future."—*Jonathan Galassi*

available through **ChelseaEditionsBooks.org** *or* **Amazon.com**